# Stop Losing Money Today

## The Art and the Science of Investing

Georges Yared

C&G Group, LLC

*This book is dedicated to my wife Cindy and to our starting five:*
*Stephanie, Ryan, Matthew, Alexandra and Joseph*

For further information, please contact:
Geoyared@aol.com

Book design by:
Arbor Books, Inc.
www.arborbooks.com

Printed in the United states

Stop Losing Money Today
Georges Yared

1. Title 2. Author 3. Investments/personal finance

Library of Congress Control Number: 2006908092

ISBN 10: 0-9789515-0-6
ISBN 13: 978-0-9789515-0-4

# Acknowledgements

I learned early on in this process that it does take a team of people to get a book to the stage of a finished product. I cannot thank enough my dear friend Dave Larue, who started working on me back in January 2006, when we were together in the mountains of Idaho. He told me time and again that I had what it took. Dave, I am forever indebted to you and your persistence.

I also have to dearly thank my three great sisters for their unwavering support and proofreading during this project. Charlette, Monique and Nicky, thanks for the love and support. Charlette was my toughest coach throughout this project and I have a feeling she will be the same for the projects to come.

My eldest daughter Stephanie served as my proofreader. She read the first draft in one day, one sitting. She has enough enthusiasm for 20 people. Thank you also to her husband Chad and my beautiful granddaughter Bailey for being part of my life.

Ryan and his beautiful wife Jessica, as well as Matthew, Alexandra and Joey, stood behind me all the way. I heard, "I am proud of you, Dad" a lot and that kept me motivated all the way through this project.

I want to thank dear friend and coach Robert Stuberg, founder and chairman of Success.com. Robert sat with me in early April with a blank sheet of paper and said, "Let's write an outline." Once that was accomplished, I realized I had a lot to share with the investing public.

Robert was with me and two fantastic people at Riverside Studios, where we recorded the book for CD and MP3 format. As a rookie in the studio, I was so grateful to Rodger Bliss and Sandra Lovee, who guided me through the new, scary process.

Both of my parents are gone, but their legacy lives on with my three sisters and me, as well as with our spouses, kids, grandkids and in-laws. I toast Joseph and Michelle Yared, two immigrants who arrived on the shores of the United States in 1954 with $140 in their pockets and built an incredible life filled with family and cherished friends. Their principals are with me always.

My dear wife and best friend Cindy: how can I ever thank you for your support and your "go get 'em" attitude? You had confidence in me from day one and I will never be able to thank you enough for the constant pats on the back. You are the love of my life.

# TABLE OF CONTENTS

# INTRODUCTION

MY NAME IS GEORGES J. YARED, and I have been in the investment business since February 1979, when a wonderful branch manager at Dean Witter Reynolds (now Morgan Stanley) named Thomas "Tim" Clark gave a 23-year-old kid a chance.

I had wanted to be a stockbroker since I was a teenager. I thought stockbrokers were so cool—they got to wear three-piece suits, they learned how to whisper and nobody could frown better.

I went to six different brokerage firms when looking to get into the business: Merrill Lynch, PaineWebber (now UBS Securities), Kidder Peabody, Shearson (now Citigroup), EF Hutton (which became Shearson and finally Citigroup) and Bache Securities (Prudential-Bache and now Wachovia Securities). All of them said "no" to me because I was too young and had no real experience.

Finally, this great gentleman hired me, probably to get me off his back since I had been calling him every day for three weeks. Tim Clark fully expected me to fail, as I was young and inexperienced. Most stockbrokers were in their mid-30s and older, but he hired me anyway, perhaps on a whim. I was tired of the interviews he put me through because, of course, I owned only one suit and wore it to each one.

But I was so determined to be successful. When I returned from my eight weeks of New York partying—I mean training, Tim and I had lunch. He told me to keep my almost bare résumé handy, as I was doomed for failure. I boldly asked him what the record was for first-year new accounts.

"In the Chicago office?" he asked.

I said, "No, the whole firm."

He told me it was 228 new accounts. I matter-of-factly told him I would break the record. He still suggested I keep my sparse résumé handy!

In my first production year at Dean Witter Reynolds, June 1979 through May 1980, I shattered the record for most new accounts. I opened 521 that first year. Fortunately, most of them were opened via telephone, so the clients never really saw how young I was! I was as green and naïve in the business as anyone, but I made up for it through dogged determination and enthusiasm.

I loved the business so much that after six months of production, Dean Witter Reynolds offered me the chance to go back to the New York training center once a month to address the classes there on "how to do it right." After three years of full-time production, I was given the chance to manage a large Dean Witter branch in Oakbrook, Illinois, and then two years later, in 1985, I was made Midwest regional manager, based in Chicago.

In that capacity, I managed and supervised almost 1,200 brokers in 40 branch offices covering 11 states. The region at that time was generating over $170 million in annual revenues. From 1987 through 1989, I had the honor of being president and CEO of Dean Witter Canada, headquartered in Toronto. We tripled the size of the firm in those two years and subsequently sold it to a large Canadian bank.

Beginning in 1992, I had the opportunity to go to the "other side" of the business when I joined investment banking research boutique firm Wessels, Arnold and Henderson, based in Minneapolis, Minnesota.

Wessels was a highly respected firm in the late 1980s all through the 1990s. The reason most have never heard of it was Wessels did not deal with the investing retail public. Our clientele were the major US and European institutions, professional money management firms and hedge funds. They valued the Wessels growth research and our sector research in technology and healthcare.

Wessels employed some world-class analysts: Tom Erickson, a major computer networking analyst; Steven Sigmond, one of the first and best Internet analysts; Peter Schleider, a renowned software analyst; David Duclos, one of the finest medical device analysts; Mitchell Bartlett, a superb retail analyst and among the first to embrace and write about e-commerce; and David Geraty, one of the two or three best restaurant analysts in the industry.

We were also heavily involved in bringing companies public (initial public offerings, or IPOs) and advising them in various capacities. I was working with our European clients in France, England and Switzerland. I advised them on their American stock portfolios. I had the privilege of working with some of the best professional portfolio managers in the world. I had a few US-based clients as well.

In my capacity, I was able to travel extensively overseas with many publicly listed American company managements. I was in a position to get to know them, advise them and understand their true values and motivations to succeed.

I got to know the CEOs and CFOs of over 125 companies—names like Parametric Technology, Synopsys Corp., Lone Star Steakhouse and Saloon, Sonic Corp., Medtronic, St. Jude Medical, Rational Software, Cisco Systems, Pure Software, Atria Systems, Steris Corp., J. Jill Fashion Group and Scimed Life, which was bought out by Boston Scientific.

3

I also had the opportunity to host a group of European portfolio managers in the San Francisco (Silicon Valley) area, visiting up to 20 companies in a week, on 55 different occasions. On these trips, we had the chance to visit companies like Cisco Systems, Oracle Software, Sun Microsystems, Ascend Communications, Genentech, Wind River Systems, BroadVision, Lycos, Symantec and about 150 more.

You learn so much more about a company when you visit it in its neighborhood because management teams tend to be a lot more relaxed and informative there.

In 1998, the partners at Wessels, Arnold and Henderson, myself included, sold our firm to Dain Rauscher Corp. and became Dain Rauscher Wessels. In 2000, it was sold to the Royal Bank of Canada, which renamed the firm RBC Dain.

It became way too large and bureaucratic for my taste, so in January 2003, I joined ThinkEquity Partners, headquartered in San Francisco. ThinkEquity is a research boutique as well, replicating some of the successful boutiques of the 1980s and 1990s such as Hambrecht & Quist, Robertson Stephens & Co., Alex. Brown & Sons, Montgomery Securities and of course, Wessels, Arnold and Henderson. ThinkEquity does first-class growth research and investment banking/advisory services.

## Why This Book?

Although I believe I have made many mistakes in my investment career, fortunately, I have been part of many more successes. I have learned what I call "the tricks of the trade."

In my career, I have worked directly with over 1,000 retail customers and with over 500 public companies. I have known over 2,000 retail stockbrokers, many superb professionals and sadly, some not so professional.

I have also had the opportunity to interact with over 5,000 retail customers in my management capacities at Dean Witter Reynolds. I had the opportunity to know over 150 research analysts and have worked directly with over 100 professional portfolio managers.

I kept a journal over the years as I encountered successful brokers, customers, research analysts, portfolio managers and public companies. I believe so much of the mystery of Wall Street really isn't so mysterious after all but can be understood through a series of calculated strategies to make investing simplified and successful.

I love this business and believe so strongly in the American system of investing and rewarding those who persevere, whether they are companies trying to grow or individual investors trying to enhance and grow their own portfolios.

The 10 chapters of this book delve into the nuts and bolts of investing, but I believe and hope the book will make it fun and fairly simple for you. Most of the terminology I use will be familiar to you, but in case it isn't, I'll often give brief definitions or, for more complete explanations, you can turn to the glossary that appears at the end of the book.

As I mentioned, there is no mystery. So much of investing is common sense, removing emotions (if possible!), asking the right questions of your adviser/broker, having the patience to see things through and doing some independent thinking.

In this book, I will teach you how to know when to buy, sell and buy more. It is part art, but also part science. I will identify some great companies to invest in. I also want to be able to drive home the difference between pure speculation and intelligent investing. The difference is enormous and important to distinguish.

Finally, there is finding your own approach, realistically understanding what your objectives are, your risk tolerance and what style suits you best. Whether you like stock mutual funds or individual stocks, be inquisitive and have fun. Hopefully, it is a long game and there will be many twists and turns along the way.

Have fun on this journey…and stop losing money today!

## CHAPTER 1

# WHEN INVESTING, DON'T
# LET EMOTIONS RULE

Two outs, bottom of the ninth inning, bases loaded and the game is tied…here's the wind up…and the pitch…it's a…

Emotions at this precise moment are running very high. Think about it—nine players in the field are completely focused on hopefully catching the last out or making that clean, accurate throw to first base for the last out.

On the other side, the batter is laser-focused on the pitcher, hoping to connect for the game-winning hit. His 3 teammates are on base, taking their leads, praying for a hit or even an error; 20 other teammates in the dugout, 40,000 fans in the stands and possibly millions watching on TV are all hoping too, with fingers crossed.

Baseball, as many have said, is designed to break our hearts. Emotions in a nine-inning game can go up and down 50 times. The rollercoaster is part of the joy of sports, whether you're participating or spectating.

Investing, however, should never be emotional. Never. In my 27 years in the industry, I sometimes feel like the wily old beat cop who has "seen it all"—and then, of course, something new happens, and I just shake my head.

In those 27 years, 13 spent on the private client side and

the last 14 advising professional portfolio managers and companies, I have seen exhilaration, anger, laughter, fist slamming, confusion, bliss and so on. I have witnessed these emotions in everyone, from the small investor with 50 shares of a company to the manager running a $9 billion portfolio.

We are human, and emotional feelings come out in all types. But keep in mind, these are companies or stock funds…these are not our children. You should be as emotionally neutral as possible. The more you remain neutral, the less your objectivity potentially gets cloudy.

Part of being as emotionally neutral as possible is not falling in love with a company. If you own stock in a company, detach yourself as best you can. I ought to know: falling in love with a company once cost me $2 million, personally.

Wait a minute, aren't I suppose to be the "professional" here, detached, removed and unemotional? Yes, but I blew it big time. Read on; this part hurts.

## *How to Lose It All*

In late 1998 and early 1999, I invested a couple hundred thousand dollars in VeriSign (ticker symbol: VRSN). VeriSign was the keeper of ."com" and ."net." All Internet addresses ending in those extensions went through the company's database.

It also sold web-based digital certificates; that is, it secured the servers that accept your private, confidential information, such as credit card numbers, email addresses and bank information so that, for example, your transaction with eBay or Amazon could be encrypted and secured.

VeriSign had a terrific business model and was the true utility of the Internet. Much of the company's revenues were on a recurring basis, meaning annual renewals; therefore, payment for .com and .net was $6 per year and the web-based certificates were $699 per server, per year. Nearly as perfect as perfect can be!

I personally got to know the CEO, Stratton Sclavos. A truly accomplished man, a lot of industry experience, very good communicator—all the right stuff. I took several professional portfolio managers to VeriSign's Silicon Valley headquarters to meet with Stratton and his team.

We toured the database facility, which is as secure as the US Pentagon data facility. It was so elaborate that even CEO Stratton could not walk in alone; he had to have an escort.

Wow, I thought. The Internet was growing like a weed, and these guys were the utility. You had to go through VeriSign to do just about anything on the Internet (which, by the way, is more true today than ever). The stock was a strong buy. I was absolutely right.

I told all my clients after they had bought shares that I was taking a personal position (full disclosure). From 1998 through 2000, my goodness, VeriSign was executing superbly. My $200,000 grew to $2.5 million—time to sell! No way. It was going to $5 million!

After all, I knew Stratton Sclavos, had dinner with him three or four times, hosted him outside Silicon Valley to visit investors, knew his kids' names, his upbringing…This was a quality guy—smart, cutting edge, innovative. I figured I could ride the VeriSign horse forever. The stock was an absolute buy and hold; never sell!

Truth is, I fell in love with a company and its management team. My judgment was totally clouded. VeriSign went on to make several expensive acquisitions, some of which were confusing and viewed as nonstrategic. The company's focus appeared blurred, investors got nervous, and the stock came down over a one-year period.

With the technology bubble-burst also acting as a catalyst, VeriSign fell to as low as $3.87 per share. Ugh! My $2.5 million was then worth only $40,000. What an idiot I had been. So many signals and red flags had been staring me in the face; I could have sold with a $2.5 million profit—or a $2 million profit, or even a $1.5 million profit—at any time.

VeriSign didn't fall overnight; it fell almost systematically over one year. There I was, advising clients on millions and billions of dollars to remain detached from the emotional involvement, but I fell right into the trap myself.

## *Getting Back on Track*

So what did I do after the stock was down to less than $4? After licking my wounds and kicking myself over and over, I put my professional hat back on!

I took some of my clients who were professional portfolio managers to visit VeriSign. We did not do dinner with Stratton, just went to the company's offices. We examined all the things nonemotional investors were supposed to: cash position, cash flow analysis, earnings model, addressable market size, current market share, competition, and so on.

Yes, my clients and I bought more shares in the $5 to $6 range, and the stock is now at $24 (at this writing), where it should be.

VeriSign and Stratton Sclavos have righted the ship and refocused the company, and they are executing it very well. As CEO, he has grown in the job and in fact is a rare breed in Silicon Valley, as he has been in the position for 11 years now.

I have had dinner with Stratton and my clients three times since the $3.87 bottom debacle. I like Stratton and admire him a great deal, but now I examine his company without emotion!

One of the cardinal rules of investing is to be as emotionally detached from your investments as possible. Even if you are a happy consumer of a particular company's products, keep a neutral outlook as you study data on an individual company or stock funds, management teams, financials and, of course, stock or stock fund prices.

But on the flip side, be aware of other people's behavior and emotions. They can be used to your advantage in making an investment decision. Watch their body language and measure their passion or lack of passion.

Case in point: In 1993, my firm, Wessels, Arnold and Henderson, was "on the cover" of the prospectus with two other investment boutiques for the IPO of Wind River Systems (WIND), a complicated technology company who, in essence, manufactured a software that enabled electrical engineers to design real-time operating systems.

An example of a real-time operating system (RTOS) would be the airbags in your car. They deploy, when necessary, in a millisecond. The RTOS in the airbag system determines if the collision and the angle of the collision merit deployment, again all in a millisecond.

Another example is the anti-lock braking system in a car. The RTOS regulates the on-and-off pressure the brakes use, even if your foot is pressed on them full-tilt. This was cutting-edge technology that brought down the cost for manufacturers to offer complex mechanical products to the masses. Wow, this stock should have been a winner from the get-go. Right? Well, read on.

## *Seeing the Signs*

The IPO roadshow went fairly well. I traveled with the company to London and my clients liked Wind River and ordered some shares for the IPO. Great.

All along, I was watching the CEO's behavior on the two-day trip, and I wasn't feeling very comfortable with him. The future and the opportunity were certainly impressive, but there was just something bizarre about the guy. He seemed confused on some accounting questions, nothing really complicated, either. He did not communicate well and seemed distracted and a bit standoffish.

These were subjective observations only. My clients didn't seem to raise any of those issue, so I thought maybe I was overreacting. Remember, although I was emotionally detached, I was taking in all the emotions around me.

On the other hand, the chairman and founder of WIND, Jerry Fiedler, was an enthusiastic, outgoing, passionate guy. He did not want the day-to-day management function; he just wanted to remain the "visionary."

Fast forward…IPO was done at $12, the stock traded up nicely for a while, but I still wasn't feeling right about the CEO. Boom! Sure enough, WIND blew a quarterly earnings expectation, lowered future earnings and revenue guidance, and the CEO (not surprisingly) resigned. Ugh!

The stock fell to $2 to $3 and, as many money managers say, "It was dead money!" Oh well, on to the next idea. Lesson learned, right?

Not so fast. I kept Wind River on my radar screen for three reasons: one, the technology was really important and cool; two, competition was at a minimum; and three, the founder and chairman was so enthusiastic and passionate. One blown quarter was not going to change that.

Six to seven months went by and as predicted, the stock was dead money. Then something hit me right between the eyes: Chairman Jerry Fiedler bought 50,000 shares of WIND in the open market (all insider transactions, buys and sells, must be reported and are public record).

He bought the shares outright for cash, not company stock options or restricted shares. I can give you 50 reasons why company managements sell shares: diversification purposes, too much of their net worth is tied up in the one company, a new house, a vacation house, a fancy new sports car, and so on.

But there is only one reason to buy, only one: that person is confident in the company and puts his money where his mouth is. So I called Jerry, and he was only too happy to talk, because Wall Street had kind of abandoned WIND and not many investors were knocking on his door to talk.

Now in my discussion with Jerry, I wasn't looking for inside information, as that is illegal (which I'll discuss in a later chapter). What I was looking for was insider insight (also discussed in a later chapter).

Jerry knew the rules and in no way would discuss what was not already public, but his emotions were very high. He was enthusiastic about current prospects for WIND and very happy about the new CEO, and I just felt that he was seeing a real turnaround in his company—and he put his money where his mouth was.

I brought four portfolio managers out to Silicon Valley to visit WIND about three weeks later. Analysts still had a "hold" rating (as opposed to buy or sell) on WIND shares, and many investors still had them in the "penalty box," as they had by then blown the last two quarters. Basically, no one cared about Wind River.

## The Right Approach

My clients were a bit reluctant to visit WIND as well. There were so many good companies in the Valley; they wondered, Why waste our time here?

My answer was, because Jerry was enthusiastic, wore his emotions on his sleeve and put his own money into the stock.

Well, the good news is, Wind River did turn around. The new CEO did a great job of reorganizing the firm and the stock has 20-folded since. RTOS is a critical application in many products in the automotive, communications and aerospace industries, and Jerry, who just retired from Wind River, is still as enthusiastic and passionate as ever.

Again, the lesson to learn is to observe other people's emotions but remain as emotionally detached as possible yourself. Whenever I watch CNBC, Bloomberg TV on the Internet, Wall Street Week or any other financial network or show, I'm looking for the management team or individual's emotions, body language and enthusiasm or lack of it.

I watch very carefully how a CEO or COO or CFO handles an interview after his or her company has blown a quarter and has reduced forward-earning guidance. Executives are a very over-lawyered group to begin with and are trained to answer interviewer questions in neutral, boring, almost noncommittal language.

Watch to see if the executive is overly defensive—for example, blaming customers, or interest rates rising, or "the economy" and my favorite, if it's a retailer, the weather. The more defensive an executive is, the more it tells me that additional bad news is coming.

If an executive appears more straight up, accepts the blame for missing expectations and does not blame others, that could indicate that the worst is behind the company. It's subjective, of course, but these people are human, tend to be competitive and driven, and want to win.

Your job is to remain as detached as possible, even if you are angry because you've lost money in the stock.

Remember, these are companies and/or stock funds…they are not our children!

## Chapter 2

# Trust...But Verify

Back in the 1980s, President Ronald Reagan was establishing a warm, friendly relationship with Soviet President Mikhail Gorbachev. The two were negotiating an arms reduction agreement and as much as they laughed, joked and just plainly got along, Reagan instructed his team to "trust…but verify."

The same holds true for you as an investor. We are in an era of information overload, between the Internet, printed financial publications, public relations-based press releases, television, cable news shows, your broker's phone calls, emails…stop this merry-go-round!

Whom should you believe? Whom should you trust? Where did all these television "experts" come from, anyway? TV commercials show you how "easy" it is to trade online. Smiling actors imitate happy, winning investors, never losing money, enjoying life. These are great images and are sometimes reality, but mostly they're just plain old nonsense.

## *Know Your Broker*

Most investors I have met—and I have met thousands—still want the human touch. They want a financial adviser, a human being who makes his or her living providing advice and counsel. In spite of the incredible technology available today, most investors want that trusted broker.

They come with many different names: financial adviser, account executive, financial representative and even financial counselor. They come with even fancier titles: assistant vice president, vice president, first vice president and the big one, senior vice president.

Let's eliminate one myth right off the bat. These fancy titles are commission production-based and earned. They are not earned by generating superior returns for their clients. They are not earned by avoiding the pitfalls for their clients. They are not earned by being emotionally detached for their clients.

These titles are awarded on commissions generation in a calendar year and/or by accumulating large numbers of clients' assets "under administration" in a calendar year.

Brokerage firm compliance departments have become enormously sophisticated in the last 10 to 15 years. The rule of thumb that compliance officers diligently watch for is what level of commissions does a broker generate from the asset base he has under administration.

The acceptable level—one that does not raise any red flags—is roughly 1 percent. So, if your broker has $50 million in clients' assets under administration, his commissions for the year should be between $450,000 and $600,000. Any commission amount above that will almost guarantee a compliance review and audit. Any number below that will merit a meeting with the broker's branch manager as to why the commission levels are so low!

I'm being a bit simplistic here, but you get the general idea. Your big-name firms compensate their advisers, financial counselors, account executives—whatever their titles—strictly on commission production. Some firms will compensate their first and second-year brokers on a salary basis and bonus them on "assets raised," but normally after three years, it is straight production pay.

Included in the commission amounts are "residuals" that many mutual fund companies "share" with the broker of record. The residuals come from the management fees that are charged to the customers or shareholders.

The residual program works as follows: you have $100,000 in a stock mutual fund, whether it be your broker's firm's fund (or family of funds) or an outside fund. Typically, the fund pays 20 to 25 basis points (1 basis point equals 0.01 percent, so 20 to 25 would be 0.20 percent to 0.25 percent) to the broker annually.

So that $100,000 balance will yield your broker a $200 to $250 payout. This does not include the initial buy commission, which can run anywhere from 2 percent up to 4½ percent. Fixed income, or bond funds, tends to pay 10 basis points of residuals. Therefore, the broker earns compensation on both "active" and idle dollars.

In the past, stockbrokers were exactly that—stockbrokers. They had specific stock and/or bond recommendations and occasionally stock and/or mutual fund ideas. With the proliferation of "financial products," today's broker is more of an "asset gatherer," recommending and placing clients' monies in different families of funds, annuities and various other products.

Basically, this has reduced the risks for most brokerage firms, as packaged products tend to be less volatile and suitability less a potential issue. It can also take a lot of the fun out of selecting good growth companies and doing one's homework.

## *Finding the One Who's Right for You*

So, how do you pick a broker/adviser? Forget the fancy titles; they're not very relevant to what you need. Sometimes a rookie or a second-year broker is more valuable than a senior vice president. Rookies will work harder and longer for their clients, and they tend to be better listeners! Many brokers hook up with a new client from a referral, a social gathering or a seminar.

As a client, remember the two cardinal rules: 1) It's your money and 2) Trust…but verify. If you are establishing a new relationship with a broker, you must interview him or her. Just as they're trying to size you up—that is, trying to figure out how much money you have and where it currently is—you must do the same thing to them.

Key questions to ask the broker are: what is your investment philosophy? Are you growth oriented or income oriented? How many clients do you have? Be reasonable with that one, though; if the broker is a rookie or in her second year, don't expect a huge number.

The next question is important because it will set the tone of what you expect: How much contact do you initiate with your clients?

These questions will start a dialogue and give you an idea of the broker's philosophy and character.

The old expression holds true here: we do business with people we like. That's fine. It's okay to like and value your broker, but remember, he or she works for you. Make absolutely sure that your broker/adviser clearly understands your needs and objectives.

For compliance and legal reasons, the broker must fill out a new account form stating your objectives, as well as other pertinent information. But, make sure this information is not forgotten once the form is filed.

It's very important to communicate—easily said and possibly cliché, but not always done. You want your broker to call you as quickly with bad news as with good news. The bad-news call is always the toughest to make, but clients I have dealt with for 27 years, both private individuals and huge institutions, want that call as quickly as the good-news call. The worst thing is to hear bad news from a third party, like the television or the Internet.

One example I will never forget happened back in the early 80s. I was a third-year broker but also assumed the responsibility of managing a small office for Dean Witter Reynolds in the northern Chicago suburbs.

I did a manager's compliance review of a particularly active account. Her name was Ingrid, a Swedish immigrant who also happened to be recently widowed. She and her broker just did not get along at all. They couldn't communicate, nor could they agree on anything.

He asked me to take over the account, which I did. I called Ingrid, introduced myself as the "branch manager" and we began our dialogue. She should have been invested in conservative stocks and bonds, but she loved to swing for the fences (a definite red flag!).

I tried to position her portfolio more conservatively and more prudently, but she'd have no part of it. She wanted the action! She was invested in a hokey stock that traded by appointment only (meaning it did not trade much volume), had no real research behind it and scared the heck out of me. Sure enough, the company blew up one afternoon—they horribly missed a quarterly earnings expectation—and the stock came down by 55 percent.

It was amazing how the "volume" showed up. I desperately

tried to reach her and let her know the bad news, but Ingrid was nowhere to be found. Her kids couldn't find her, her mother didn't know where she was…she was just gone.

Finally, three days later, she called me screaming her lungs out: "Why didn't you call?" I told her I tried, that I spoke to her kids and her mother. After her tirade, I learned she had been in Las Vegas, gambling away like crazy. She was mad that I didn't find her. In fact, she was madder about our not communicating than about the stock being down!

Amazingly, she made up her stock loss with her Las Vegas winnings. But remember, I had bad news, I desperately tried to reach her and couldn't and she was more upset that we "didn't talk." I subsequently closed her account and she moved it to another firm where "they promised to talk to her more often." Good luck, Ingrid!

### *You Get What You Ask For*

Another thing that you should do when interviewing a new broker, even though it can sometimes be uncomfortable, is ask for three to five referrals. Obviously, the broker will give you the names of a few happy clients, and that's fine, but also ask for two or three unhappy or departed clients.

If the broker balks or hesitates here, just ask what happened. Why did he lose those clients? Half the time it's the client's fault—that is, there was a personality conflict, time constraints, lack of understanding or lack of communication, all of which are plausible.

The point here is to let the broker know right away that you want and need communication.

You should call the "happy" three to five references not to be nosy, but to understand the broker's modus operandi and philosophy. It's amazing the information that happy clients will give you.

You do not need to ask about investment performance, although many will volunteer it, nor are you trying to play a game of "gotcha." You just want to know if these happy clients are getting enough communication and if their objectives are being met and understood. Again, the broker may be a nice, personable person, so trust…but verify.

As for research analysts and research departments, here is where "trust…but verify" is critical. Your broker calls you and says that his or her firm's analyst really likes ABC Corp. It's about $20 per share and they expect good earnings results.

Typically, the client's response is, "Well, if you think it's okay and your analyst likes it, then I guess it's okay." I have heard that response thousands upon thousands of times.

Stop! The following method takes exactly five minutes to implement and, more importantly, puts you and your broker on the same page. It may also save you a lot of money!

The first question you need to ask—and I can assure you your broker is not expecting it (again, you are not playing gotcha; you just want to make sure she is thinking and working hard for you) is, "Tell me about this analyst."

Follow it up with these questions: how timely have this analyst's last five recommendations been? What about the analyst's timing of buy to hold or hold to buy in the last five recommendations? For the idea you are recommending now, is the analyst early or just following the Street? How accurate has the analyst been on this company the last four to six quarters? (That is, has the analyst been accurate in forecasting earning expectations?)

If this is a new recommendation, meaning the analyst has not published on this company before, ask if the analyst follows the competitors to this company. If so, then repeat the same questions above.

Also, ask if this analyst has an "initiation" piece written and have it sent to you. The idea here is, although you may not read it, you want to make sure your broker does.

The point is to make sure your broker is doing his or her homework. When something goes wrong with a company, the easiest thing to do—and I have seen it done thousands of times—is to blame the analyst. But if you and your broker can flush out the past success, or lack thereof, money can be saved.

More questions to ask are as follows: how long has your analyst been publishing? How many companies does the analyst cover and publish on? Is the analyst's background from industry or from the MBA track, and he or she just happens to like this industry? (I'll take an analyst from industry almost every time.)

Does the analyst have an industry theme piece? This is important because you want an analyst who has an industry theme, a thesis regarding the direction or growth of a particular industry, who the key players are and what paradigm shift is occurring in the industry.

If the analyst has an industry theme piece, ask to have it sent to you. I can assure you that if your broker mails it to you, she will also read it.

## Analysts Versus Reporters

The idea here is that not all analysts are created equal. Many are absolutely superb, ahead of the curve and can see their industry shifting, new players emerging, new technologies replacing old industry titans and so on.

Example: in the 1990s to early 2000s, Thomas Erickson of Wessels, Arnold and Henderson (which, as I've said before, later became Dain Rauscher Wessels and then RBC Dain) was one of the top—if not the premier—networking analysts in the world.

Tom followed names like Cisco Systems (CSCO), Wellfleet (WFLT), Chipcom (CHPM), and so on. In the early 90s, he authored a research piece titled "The Big Switch." It became the "go to" reference piece on what was to come in the networking world.

Tom was way ahead of the curve, predicting and forecasting the critical trends and who the players would be. He subsequently authored three more "Big Switch" pieces that accurately laid out the networking world.

Other analysts are what we call "reporters." They report the news about a company or an industry but are not in front of the curve. Example: many good analysts follow Wal-Mart (WMT), and publishing on Wal-Mart is a fairly simple process. There is nothing really new that any one analyst has identified, and Wal-Mart has a history of being tight-lipped with the Street about intra-quarterly updates.

No analyst is going to distinguish his or her career by publishing a quarterly note on Wal-Mart's quarterly earnings release. We can all read it on the various news services. It is plain and simple "maintenance" research.

But it is necessary to follow Wal-Mart as an industry backdrop to understand the dynamic growth of Costco (COST) or the execution issues of Kohl's (KSS). Publishing on Costco can distinguish an analyst because not all analysts agree on the growth rate, the business model and the earnings leverage forecasting the next two to three years. This is where real research can and should be done.

Another example is the semiconductor space. Intel (INTC) is a mammoth company with huge consumer recognition. The commercials for many personal computers—Dell, Compaq and IBM—all have the line, "Intel Inside."

Intel is a leader in so many areas of the semiconductor space, it is the barometer for the group. Most semiconductor analysts who follow Intel have similar current ratings (buy, hold or sell) and are all within two or three cents of each other in earnings forecasts for this year and next. Pure maintenance research.

Intel dictates very tightly to the Street its information flow and no one analyst has a differing or distinguishable opinion of them. So where is the value add? The same analysts who follow Intel can distinguish themselves on the smaller semiconductor plays where opinions, timing and earnings expectations will vary.

What are the analysts saying about Xilinx (XLNX), Alterra (ALTR), MIPS (MIPS), Intersil (ISIL) and Sandisk (SNDK)? This is where the good analysts are separated from the "reporters."

## Is Your Broker Hearing You?

As a client, you need to know if your broker's recommendation has any real teeth to it or not. Ask questions, ask questions, ask questions! By doing this, you will help make your broker better prepared to deal with you, and you will make him or her accountable. They will know that they'll have to do their homework before making any future recommendations to you.

By asking all the previously mentioned questions, the monitoring of the investment becomes a natural side effect. If there's pertinent changing news, good or bad, you will get a call with an explanation. It's all part of the understanding and communication set up in the very beginning of the relationship.

One note of advice to you, the client: if your broker truly does the homework and has your best interests at heart, pay him. This is not the time to ask for a discount. Pay for the work. Thoughtful and thorough research can help you make a fortune. Don't get hung up on the commission or fee rate.

Also, once you have accepted a recommendation, with all

the homework and analysis performed, accept responsibility for the investment. I cannot tell you how many times I have had to arbitrate a "client complaint" when, in fact, there should have been no complaint at all. The idea was discussed, dissected and monitored. It was no one's fault—it just did not work out for whatever number of possible reasons.

I have also arbitrated a number of times when the common complaint was, "I didn't understand what I bought." Here is when compliance and branch managers go ballistic because there is a total lack of communication. Either the broker was at fault for "not knowing his or her customer," or the client held back important information regarding objectives, risk tolerance and so on.

I cannot stress enough the importance of talking to, listening to and understanding each other. I've seen so many situations where if a little communication had taken place, complaints would never have surfaced because all parties would have been on the same page.

Remember: trust…but verify.

## CHAPTER 3

# PATIENCE!

THE TOUGHEST PART OF INVESTING is having the patience to wait it out. It can be frustrating and sometimes, very emotional. (Remember: detach your emotions; these are investments, not our children.)

I cannot tell you how many thousands of times I've heard "Man, what's taking so long?" Or the best one, the one that makes me question my sanity: "Are you sure about this?"

Admittedly, it's frustrating to have done all the homework on a company or a stock fund and then watch it materialize slowly—sometimes very slowly! Of course, what's even worse is when you're wrong and the idea tanks.

## *What Type of Investor Are You?*

Now, here is the question I love, and brokerage firms must ask it for legal and compliance reasons: are you a short-term investor or a long-term investor? The answer should always be, "I'm an investor, period."

You want well thought-out investment recommendations, with definitive price targets (which I'll discuss in a later chapter).

If the recommendation happens to work out in six months, I guess I'm a short-term investor. But if the idea should take 14 months to work out, I guess I'm a long-term investor. By the way, if the idea works out or tanks in three days, I'm a trader!

You are placing your hard-earned money into the stock of a company that you, or you and your broker plus the analyst, feel is going to appreciate in value. You obviously want those dollars to be worth more in the future than they are today. You hope that the company you've invested in earns more in the future, making the enterprise more valuable. Simple enough.

But what about patience? You want action now. The market is moving up, but your stock or fund is not participating, or not participating enough. The market is moving down, and your stock or fund is moving down faster.

This is why you need to be communicating with your broker. Are the story—the what, how, why and the possible future of the business—and the fundamentals still intact? Have there been any changes within the industry—meaning does someone have a better mousetrap? Or, are we early?

Great investors have been known to be patient and consistent. Examining the track record of Warren Buffett and his company Berkshire Hathaway, we see that he and his company have been exactly that. Buffett has a portfolio of mainstream, some would say boring, companies. Yet, they lead their particular industries, have excellent management and execute superbly.

Buffet's owned the stocks of a carpet company, insurance and reinsurance companies and consumer staples like Gillette and Coca-Cola. There have been years when the Berkshire portfolios have underperformed vis-à-vis the general market, and years when they have far outperformed it. Some sectors got hot while others, for no apparent reason, were cold. (Sector rotation will be covered later.)

## *Patience Pays Off*

Let me give you an example of patience. In July 1996, my firm, Wessels, Arnold and Henderson, was involved with the IPO underwriting of BroadVision (BVSN), a technology company located in Silicon Valley. The founder and CEO, Pehong Chen, was a passionate and futuristic-thinking technologist and CEO, and a real gentleman.

He was also on the board of directors of Seibel System (SEBL, recently bought out by Oracle Corp), a cutting-edge software company in the CRM (customer relationship management) space. BroadVision, to make it simple, helped companies design their websites and included a whole host of technical functions for them, including intranets and extranets. Remember now, this was 1996.

The IPO roadshow went well, but professional investors were a bit reticent because BroadVision was not yet profitable and the story was a bit difficult to understand. The IPO filing range was $8 to $10 per share. July 1996 was also a tough technology market environment, so the appetite for BroadVision was tepid at best.

I had a British client, Duncan Byatt, who at the time worked for Gartmore Investments. He loved the story and was very impressed with Pehong Chen. But Duncan also realized that the "technology tape" (tech stocks as a whole) was sloppy and that BroadVision was indeed probably coming to the market a bit early.

Duncan saw the future and realized this was probably a big idea. Savvy as he was (and still is—Duncan today runs and owns Eagle & Dominion Asset Management in London), he ordered 800,000 shares at $7 per share, all or none. The IPO was filed for 4 million shares, so Duncan was prepared to "take down" (own) 20 percent of the underwriting.

As the "order" book was slow to come together, Duncan

knew he would get all 800,000 shares, but he also served as the catalyst; he was the "anchor order" that the underwriters could point to, thus causing other clients to be quickly interested. Duncan not only anchored the deal, but he set the price at $7. It was a discount to the filing range of $8 to $10, but hey, times were tricky! He did get all 800,000 shares.

Duncan Byatt ran the growth funds at Gartmore and was accustomed to getting performance in rather short order. I asked him why he was doing this one, as we both knew that once it was public, the stock was probably going to be "quiet money"—few people would be buying or selling it.

His explanation was superb and thought provoking. He really believed that BroadVision was going to be a big idea with huge performance, and when the Street woke up to it and the leadership of Pehong Chen, professional portfolio managers would have a hard time building proper size positions (buying shares) without driving the shares way up.

He was right. BroadVision was indeed priced at $7 per share and for two years, the stock traded in a narrow range of $6 to $8. Boring, tedious and "are we sure about this one" were mentioned many times by many people. Duncan never wavered once; he even added shares when there were impatient sellers around.

The company was almost ignored. At brokerage firm growth conferences, BroadVision always got the dreaded 3:30 p.m. time slot to present its story—it's a deadly time at conferences because most professional portfolio managers are already on the golf course! The "hot" companies and stories always get the time slots before lunch.

To make the story more interesting, in early November 1998, I took legendary British portfolio manager Dr. Michael Mullaney of Threadneedle Investments to Silicon Valley to visit about 20 companies in 5 days. Mike thought I was nuts to put BroadVision on the schedule, but I hoped that 2 important things were going to happen that were critical to putting the company into the mainstream.

First, I was pretty sure that in the December quarter (ending December 31, 1998), BroadVision would actually turn a small profit. Second, if that happened, BroadVision would appear on many new "radar" screens. Once a company actually reports an operating profit, many funds that cannot invest in unprofitable companies take instant notice.

Pehong Chen welcomed us with open arms and a one-hour scheduled meeting actually turned into three hours. Pehong diligently explained the marketplace, BroadVision's positioning and the opportunity that was ahead of them. It was fabulous. This was early November 1998, a full two months before the quarter was to end.

Wall Street estimates called for breakeven and possible profitability in the March quarter (ending March 31, 1999). Pehong would not comment on the December quarter except for the lawyer-advised, "We are comfortable with Street expectations." But Mike and I could tell that something was brewing.

Michael Mullaney began to accumulate shares in November and December totaling 1.6 million shares. He bought them patiently and with strict limits.

Sure enough, BroadVision went from a loss to turning a profit, and the December quarter came through with one penny per share of earnings! BroadVision did indeed hit the mainstream, and over the next three years we saw the stock explode by nearly 80 times.

Both Duncan and Michael have told me it was their biggest winner ever. Both showed enormous patience and diligence. They understood the story and the opportunity at hand, and they waited it out.

They also understood how the other fund managers would migrate to BroadVision's story and growth opportunities. By the way, at the ensuing growth conferences sponsored by investment banking research boutique firms like Wessels, Arnolds and Henderson, Robertson Stephens & Co. and Alex. Brown Inc., Pehong got the coveted 9:00 a.m. time slot to present his story!

For nearly two and a half years, BroadVision did nearly nothing. It seeded its marketplace, won customers over and built its business. Few investors really cared at the time. Those who were patient and understood BroadVision's vision were hugely rewarded.

There are some great stories here and coming in 2006 and 2007, some big ideas. Opsware (OPSW—I'll discuss them in the next chapter) is one that some portfolio managers have owned (as do I) for the past year and a half. Performance has been minimal, but the company is going "mainstream" and has a brilliant future.

Some other big ideas in this marketplace are names like Costco (COST). Straight up, Costco is eating Sam's Club (of Wal-Mart) for lunch. It has superior execution, a great shopping experience and club membership in which renewals are very high and at higher rates. Costco is one-ninth the size of Wal-Mart in market-capitalization terms, but growing like a weed.

## *Building…Nurturing…Growing*

Wealth is built over time. As you look at building yours through individual stocks, stock funds or both, approach it in a patient, long-term manner.

Wealth is built in equities (stocks or funds) and not in bonds, corporate, government or municipals. Bonds will give you current income with some fluctuation in underlying value, but they will never provide you with wealth accumulation or asset growth. Bonds in your portfolio should provide a stream of current income and may be important in retirement, but even then, growth should still be an important component.

The following story really illustrates this point. In 1979, I was a rookie retail broker with Dean Witter Reynolds in Chicago. The company was offering its employees a retirement savings plan (not yet titled 401(k)—and what does that "k" stand for, anyway?). We could put in up to 10 percent of our earnings and the firm would match us 30 cents on the dollar. I was a 24-year-old rookie but I figured, if not now, when?

So, I maxed it out. My assistant Linda (don't be impressed, she also assisted five other brokers), who was the same age as me, laughed when I suggested she do the same. After all, we were 40 years away from retiring. Plus, she was a real consumer of clothes, travel and so on.

I finally convinced her to put one percent of her earnings in the plan. I told her, "Just do a lousy one percent. It's a start, and you'll never miss the money. And put it into the growth fund—never, ever the fixed income funds."

She agreed and after one year, she raised her contribution to three percent of her earnings.

Fast forward…in 2005, both Linda and I turned 50 years old (ouch!). It was a milestone. Sadly, Linda's husband died suddenly last year, leaving her with two teenagers to raise. About a month after her husband's funeral, she called me up to wish me a happy 50th birthday, and to thank me.

Thank me for what? Linda was still with Morgan Stanley (Dean Witter's name change due to a merger with Morgan Stanley), she earned roughly $100,000 per year and stunningly, her 401(k) just crossed over the $1 million mark! I was both floored and elated for her.

She thanked me for pestering her 25 years earlier and in fact, she had joined the plan just to get me off her back! After five years, she upped her contributions to eight percent and she has kept at that level ever since—and stayed in the growth funds!

She was tempted several times during the years to move her money to the fixed income fund because of world events, political events, the crash of 1987, the mini-crash of 1989, the 1998 Asian currency crisis, Iraq I and Iraq II, nuclear fears, the fall of the Berlin Wall and, of course, 9/11/01, but she stayed the course in growth.

She got really excited when I told her that the money should grow to between $3 million and $4 million by her 65th birthday!

Patience! Linda earned a good living over the years and kept salting away a portion of it, and look at the results.

## *Start Slow, End Big*

The news can be frightening and challenging, but the economy continues to grow over time. Businesses are built to grow and to grow their profits.

We have our hiccups, always will, but plow ahead and be patient. If you have young children or grandchildren, set up that 529 college savings fund, even if the monthly amounts are only $50 or $100. Put that money in the growth fund offering of the 529 plan and leave it alone!

Make sure you take full advantage of your employer's 401(k) plan or your IRA plan. They are certainly tax advantaged, but remember: growth funds only. You won't miss the money you contribute. Simply pretend it does not exist. That's what Linda did over the years. Her philosophy was that the money "simply did not exist; it wasn't mine"—and now she has more than $1 million.

I hear so often, "Well, the market is tough" or "This is not the right time." It's all nonsense. I cannot tell you what the stock market will do for the rest of 2006, or for 2007, but I will categorically guarantee you that the value of American companies (worldwide as well) will be significantly higher in 5, 10, 15 and 20 years. Guaranteed.

Oh sure, we'll experience some frightening, ugly events, no doubt, but as always, we will marshal through them and be more prosperous. We will see new enterprises that don't even exist today, at least not in the public markets, that will emerge as the new leaders in their fields. There will be new members of the Fortune 1000 and the S&P 500.

After all, two new members of the S&P 500 in 2006, VeriSign and Google, did not even exist 12 years ago!

Patience!

## CHAPTER 4

# THINK INDEPENDENTLY...BUT INVESTIGATE

HOW MANY TIMES HAVE YOU SEEN a new business in your neighborhood or city and said, "Gee, why didn't I think of that?"

The stock market is a collection of companies many others "thought of," and then they acted on those thoughts or visions. The beauty of the stock market is that you can join and own many of these wonderful ideas early in their life cycles.

Be an independent thinker about businesses and new concepts. Sometimes the concept is so simple, our first thought is, That'll never work, or, It's good, but there are no real barriers to entry and the competition would be heavy. The more skeptical will often think, If it's that good, why hasn't someone else done it?

## *Innovation Is the Key*

In 1987, my wife Cindy and I were on vacation in Europe. While in Paris, Cindy observed that the French love their coffee, drinking it four to five times a day. She said to me that we should move there and set up little coffee shops or stands by the subway stations and sell different types of coffee. I remember thinking, That's easy…in fact, it's so easy, it probably wouldn't work.

Anybody ever hear of Starbucks?!

Starbucks (SBUX), a $28 billion market capitalization company (market cap is all the outstanding shares multiplied by the current price), dominates the coffee space and will continue to do so. I predict they will be even bigger than McDonald's.

Remember how McDonald's started? Another "easy" idea thought up in 1955 by 54-year-old Ray Kroc. I remember him saying people thought he was nuts, he was losing it. After all, why, at 54 years old, would someone want to create a new business, and one that was so simple? People buying burgers, fries and a drink, and taking them away in their cars? It would never work. No way.

Yet Ray Kroc had the vision and the independent thinking to follow his gut, and the rest is history. The concept has been validated by the competition that followed McDonald's, such as Wendy's (WEN), Burger King (soon to be public) and the other winner in this overcrowded space, Sonic (SONC).

Independent thinking, coupled with—and this is critical—great execution, yields great businesses. Sometimes they will go full circle: they'll be created, be exciting, execute superbly, have some growing pains, dominate their markets or their niches and then some, sadly, will blow up. The question is, will they blow up temporarily, repair what went wrong and come back strong? Or will they blow up permanently?

Anybody remember Sears? Yes, a comeback story for sure. Anybody remember Montgomery Ward? Gone forever. Remember Borland and Novell? Floundering the last seven to eight years, and so far going nowhere.

The fun part is catching these stories as early as you can. Remember the discussion on BroadVision? It took independent thinking, forward vision and of course, execution on the part of management. The rewards were huge and gratifying.

Keep in mind that the majority of brokerage firm research departments are sorely lacking in the ability to predict the winners of tomorrow. The Fortune 1000 companies have an abundance of research analysts covering and publishing on them under their brokerage firm headings, but what really distinguishes and separates them?

Not much. One might be a bit earlier than another in moving a rating from buy to hold or hold to buy, but in reality not much more than that. I think at last count, 33 firms publish on Intel (INTC), Microsoft (MSFT), Wal-Mart (WMT) or General Electric (GE).

Where is the value add? The cutting edge? These giant companies are covered to the point where there are few, if any, surprises. When there is something new, all 33 firms have it at the same time. Yet these Fortune 1000 companies contribute massively to employment and benefits, and they pay huge sums in federal and local taxes!

## Investing in Independent Thinkers

Where are tomorrow's winners, and how do you find them? Where are the independent thinkers? All around us!

Let's start by taking a look at the different mutual fund families' Websites, such as those for Fideltiy and Vanguard. Click on their small-cap fund(s) and scope out the portfolios. (Large-cap means a market capitalization of more than $10 billion; mid-cap is $2 billion to $10 billion; small-cap is below $2 billion; and micro-cap is below $500 million. These ranges are an estimate, as different portfolio managers can define them a bit differently, but these are a "consensus.")

Typically, mutual funds update their portfolios at least quarterly, if not monthly. Look at the stocks in the portfolio under $1 billion market cap. Also, look at the growth portfolios that are not necessarily under $1 billion market cap. Independent thinking or sometimes well thought-out gut feelings can point to a mid-cap or even a large-cap name.

Example: out of favor right now, at least with the hot money crowd, are eBay and Amazon. Both have been amazing growth names, dominant players in basically new fields. Both have encountered growing pains in the last one to two years. These are passionate management teams, totally ahead of the curve but adjusting their business models to accommodate the changing markets and competition.

Amazon has had to build huge "bricks and mortar" distribution warehouses and make enormous technology investments to stay ahead of the pack. It has been done, and the leverage in their model looks terrific going forward.

Not many analysts will move to that "buy rating" until they see confirmation for one or two quarters' results. By that time, you will have missed the first 30 to 40 percent of price movement. Those with the gut feeling, the independent thinking, will be there early.

I don't know if Jeff Bezos, CEO of Amazon, sleeps more than four hours a day. Same with eBay: CEO Meg Whitman is a visionary, yet she possesses great execution skills.

Whenever I'm in London visiting clients, I typically stay at the Marriott Park Lane Hotel. Being a frequent guest, I've gotten to know the managers, the clerks and the maids. Great hotel, great service.

In late 2005, the general manager approached me and asked if I could spend half an hour with a special visitor, Chairman and CEO J. Willard (Bill) Marriott. He was touring the various hotels in Europe and wanted to speak with frequent guests. I agreed immediately, as I was thinking about this book and independent thinking was on my mind.

Bill Marriott, age 73, could be relaxing at a golf course somewhere, not worrying about the towels in someone's room. Instead, he was asking me insightful questions about the hotel, its service, guest comfort, and many other topics. What was interesting was that he was taking copious notes, asking follow-up questions and shaking or nodding his head a lot.

I took the occasion to ask him, "Why are you still doing this?"

He laughed and said plainly and sincerely, "'Cause I love it and I want us to be the best. Period. Nothing gives me greater pleasure than to know we are exceeding expectations."

Bill Marriott interviewed eight guests that day, and his key question to all of us was, "Tell me how we can be better— better than our competition, better than anyone else in the business."

Interestingly, he also asked, "Can you detect our Marriott culture within our staff?" What a funny, startling question. Marriott is huge on company culture. All employees are truly valued—just ask any of them. They have loyalty and passion that are rare among big companies.

The bartender at the Park Lane had written Mr. Marriott a letter with several suggestions on how to make the bar more efficient and thus more profitable. He was encouraged to do this by his general manager! No politics there!

Bill wrote him back and had two of the bartender's ideas implemented systemwide. Wow—no ego, no politics. Great teamwork led to independent thinking about how to make Marriott hotels more efficient and profitable. What an incredible culture.

## *Finding the Good Ideas of Tomorrow*

Michael Moe, founder and chairman of ThinkEquity Partners (my company), has coined the expression, "Finding the stars of tomorrow…today."

Where do you look for them? Where do you find them? The newer investment banking boutiques specialize in that search, so try to sweet-talk a research assistant at ThinkEquity Partners, JMP Securities, Pacific Crest, Pacific Growth, Roth Capital and Merriman Curhan Ford to get you on their email research distribution list, or at least to email you the list of presenting companies at their once or twice-a-year growth conferences.

Always remember that at these conferences, the really good stories present before lunch. The stories that have encountered difficulties, that are "no longer hot," present after lunch. But, by the way, that's where the opportunities may be the best. Out-of-favor companies have been through the wringer, hopefully making their management teams savvier and wiser.

BroadVision and Wind River Systems were getting used to the 3:00 or 3:30 p.m. time slot. Normally the room was fairly empty, which gave those who did not have golf games the real opportunity and time to talk to the management teams—to find out what went wrong and, more importantly, what was being done to right the ship.

Many of these conference presentations are available on company Websites, so the individual investor has as much opportunity to hear a company's presentation as the professional portfolio manager.

Where is the independent thinking today? One area is nanotechnology, an incredible world of small (no pun intended), mostly private companies that will indeed change the world. The best company to research is Harris and Harris (TINY), which is a publicly traded company holding several private venture investments in the nano world.

The company's portfolio is a true approximation of what is hopefully coming to the public markets in the field. The nano applications are numerous: medical devices, aerospace, consumer products and many more. In fact, a pair of pants or a necktie treated with a nano shield will resist coffee or even red wine poured on it. It just runs right off. (Interesting trick to play at a party!)

Another area is Internet advertising and marketing. It's amazing how many dollars are spent on traditional media like television, newspapers, magazines and radio while the Internet is commanding only about six to seven percent of those dollars.

However, that is changing in lightning-quick fashion. When Procter and Gamble (PG), the biggest producer of consumer staples, declared in 2005 that it was accelerating its spending of marketing and advertising dollars on advertising on the Internet, it woke up the Fortune 1000 in a hurry. Ford Motors launched a new pickup truck last year with all of its advertising budget spent on the Internet!

The marketing and advertising campaign leaders in this very new field are companies like aQuantive (AQNT), Digitas (DTAS) and 24/7 Real Media (TFSM). Their business models are built for the Internet; they have no legacy of traditional advertising clients that they have to "work out of." They are emerging as the go-to companies to build campaigns and they have the technology to analyze the effects of those campaigns.

## Be a Creative Thinker

Whatever it is you like, investigate it for yourself. Your gut feeling is worth more than you know. Be creative and think outside the box.

Example: with the nation at virtually full employment, I love the concept of on-site day care. Many companies outsource this vital need—check out Bright Horizons Family Solutions (BFAM).

Many employers and insurance companies also help subsidize health club memberships as healthcare costs continue to escalate. "Prevention" is finally an acceptable medical term! Check out Bally Total Fitness (BFT) on that front.

Here is another example of being early but thinking independently that I hope will pay off handsomely. Skin cancer is the most common and, fortunately, the most curable of cancers. However, dermatologists want to biopsy anything suspicious on a patient's skin—as they should.

This procedure is a bit painful and fairly expensive. Electro-Optical Sciences (MELA) is one to one and a half years away from having an FDA-approved device that will allow the dermatologist to examine a lesion or suspicious skin growth without performing a biopsy. This is potentially huge!

If and when approved, this breakthrough device will save a lot of time and money for the patient and the insurance companies, but more importantly, it will increase the accuracy of detecting a cancerous lesion. It is amazing technology with a huge addressable market.

Stock is very quiet here, around $5 a share, and very few brokerage firms follow MELA, but if and when FDA approval arrives, you can be sure many firms will provide research coverage. But many independent thinkers will already be involved with the stock!

These examples may be obvious, like adding one and one to get two. Many great ideas you cannot see or use personally, but they are out there. Many times technology is "back of the office," so it is impossible to see consumer applications. But they are critical and vital to helping organizations build better, more efficient and more cost-effective products.

## *A Personal Experience*

Independent thinkers will ask questions of people in many different fields, which is how I discovered Opsware. I heard about it from an information technology (IT) specialist friend of mine. The story is worth detailing.

I discovered this company before my firm ever published on it. I believe five or six brokerage firms now write on OPSW. Great. Bring 'em on!

My friend mentioned this new cutting-edge way to service the server world. After my head stopped spinning, I asked, "What does all that mumbo jumbo mean?"

Well, you may have heard the name Marc Andreessen. Back in the mid-80s, Marc was credited with co-inventing the Internet browser while he was a student at the University of Illinois. He then went on to co-found Netscape with venture backer Jim Clark. It was one of the first great IPOs of the 1990s.

Eventually, Netscape was acquired by AOL and Marc was given a nonsense post, one clearly not taking advantage of his remarkable skills. So he left AOL wealthy, but certainly not professionally satisfied.

Fast forward to 2001. Marc is chairman of a company called Loudcloud that went public, which came down with a loud bang! It was one of the last before we entered the nuclear winter for technology IPOs.

For reasons not important here, Loudcloud sold its Web hosting business to Electronic Data Systems (EDS) but retained an incredibly valuable piece of technology and changed its name to Opsware. Opsware is the leader in server automation.

You ask, "What does this mean?"

Servers hold all the applications that run a company, like payroll, e-mail, human resources, Websites and so on. A company like General Motors may have 70,000 to 75,000 servers; in fact, they are aptly named "server farms."

The biggest expense incurred by large companies is maintaining and updating their servers. Typically it is done manually and is therefore labor-intensive and expensive. Server farms usually receive services such as updating security patches, changing applications as they are developed and so on. Again, both time and labor intensive.

Enter Opsware. Its product is software-based server automation. Wow! That is huge! Imagine updating 10,000 servers in 24 hours instead of 24 days! Think of the labor savings—not to mention saving on human error because the process is so precision-based.

Great. It is still the first inning of a nine-inning game. Opsware's product is expensive—about $1,500 per server, per year—and is really only relevant for big server farms. A small business with 8 to 10 servers still does it manually, and it is still more cost-efficient this way.

So the Opsware customers are big; therefore, the sales and decision cycles are slow and long. CIOs of large organizations want to see demonstrations and feasibility studies before committing to a new technology, especially one that "touches" the critical applications of their company.

CFOs want to see the dollars and cents of such a large undertaking before committing millions to a project, especially for new technology that most of them do not understand. The commitment to Opsware product is expensive and lengthy, and once a company adopts Opsware product, changing it is almost impossible.

Cutting edge? Yes. Mass adoption? Not yet. Getting there? Absolutely. In addition, Opsware has introduced a "mid- market" product so companies can try it one department at a time and save on the upfront cost. They're seeding the market with smaller initial expense to its customers, but hooking them on the drug. This takes time, but the results are coming in very well.

Opsware also acquired a small private company, Rendition

Networks, which has products for networking equipment like all those Cisco switches and routers. In calendar year 2003, Opsware generated $18 million of revenues; in 2004, $37 million; in 2005, $58 million; and expectations for 2006 and 2007, respectively, are $95 million and $130 million. Both are rather conservative estimates, and the company has just crossed into profitability.

Competition is minimal and has no visible traction. Wow, do I like this story.

## *Do Your Homework*

Back to independent thinking. This story has required patience because the stock has been range bound between $5 and $9 a share these past 2½ years. The market capitalization is about $800 million, cash on the balance sheet is over $100 million and we are just getting past what we call the "missionary sales" part of their history, meaning that customers are now calling Opsware rather than Opsware "evangelizing like missionaries" to gain traction in the marketplace.

Clearly, Opsware is on the runway to higher revenues, profitability, customer loyalty and longevity—and a higher stock price.

The message here is that I believed (and still do) in Marc Andreessen. The guy was a rock star until AOL miscast him. Here is a man with something to prove—to Wall Street, to the technology world and maybe to himself. He is building what could be the next Oracle, or the next Siebel Systems or the next BEA Systems.

Opsware has the potential to be a huge stock, a game-changing player in the software/server world. On the surface, a quick glance at Opsware three years ago would have scared anyone away: it wasn't profitable and it had long, tedious sales cycles.

But with independent thinking, and using gut feelings to understanding the main man's motivation, I discovered that the idea was worth really exploring, albeit early. Now, five or six firms cover Opsware, and soon that will be up to 10 firms or more. Great. The more the merrier.

There are other Opswares out there. Think outside the box, run with your instincts—but investigate. Do your homework; ask your broker to do his or her homework as well. Ask questions of people you know who are in different industries: What's new in your world? What's coming to change your industry? What new technology do you see out there?

Think independently and listen to your spouse—as I wish I had!

## CHAPTER 5

## KNOWING WHEN TO BUY

THE NEXT THREE CHAPTERS—Knowing When to Buy, Knowing When to Sell and Knowing When to Buy More— will have several intertwining ideas.

With more than 5,000 companies publicly traded in the United States stock market and data whirring by at almost the speed of light, the great, $64,000 question is: When should you buy? (Deciding what to buy will be covered in later chapters.)

There are key questions that all investors, private individuals and professional portfolio managers must ask themselves and their brokers. Let's review them, as they are all important and should be combined to "make" the story.

### *Start With the People*

First, and probably the most important, is the management team. Who is running the company? What is the experience level of the CEO? Is his or her background in sales and marketing, research and development background or accounting and finance?

Knowing the different backgrounds can give you some

insight into the way CEOs manage and run the firms. Did the they work their way up from the mailroom? If relatively new with the company, where were they before this job? The CEO sets the tone and the direction, and should be able to communicate the vision of the company to both shareholders and employees.

The CFO should be able to communicate the vision as well but must also be able to discipline the organization financially. The CFO typically has an accounting and finance background to begin with but should also have experience managing a team of number crunchers.

The CFO is vital in communicating with shareholders and analysts, not letting "the numbers" get too far ahead of themselves. The CEO shares the overall vision; the CFO shares the "how do we get there financially?" vision.

Great companies are led by great management teams and can be destroyed by mediocre management teams. Conversely, a mediocre company can be turned around by a strong management team.

Some terrific CEOs of the past 5 to 15 years, leading and sustaining their companies through both good and lean times, include Jack Welch of General Electric (GE); Aart de Geus of Synopsys (SNPS); Howard Schultz of Starbucks (SBUX); Carol Bartz of Autodesk (ADSK); William George, recently retired from Medtronic (MDT); Steve Ballmer of Microsoft (MSFT); and John Chambers of Cisco Systems (CSCO), to name a few.

In contrast to these great leaders, I know of one CEO whose ego is in the way; he cannot lead a team or share, let alone define a vision. This man's company has so underperformed these past four years that it is now desperately acquiring other software companies to make up for a horrible research and development (R&D) program these past four to five years. Enough said.

## *Market Sizes, Growth Rates and Valuation*

So, number one is management team. Number two is, what is the addressable market size where this company plays? Sounds simple, but some companies play in a smaller industry and the game is more of market share dominance and taking additional share from competitors, if possible.

For example, Synopsys (SNPS) is one of the two leading companies in electronic design automation (EDA). SNPS will do about $1 billion in revenues this year and $1.15 billion in revenues next year. Sounds okay so far, but the EDA addressable market is only $5 billion in total size and growing maybe 7 to 9 percent per year. So, SNPS's mission is to maintain share and capture additional share in a relatively small industry with a single-digit growth rate.

Compare this with Google (GOOG) in the Internet search engine field, where the market size is massive, almost impossible to measure. Google has enjoyed triple-digit growth for the past two years and it will see at least 50 to 60 percent for the next 3 years. The Internet advertising/media space has a current addressable market size of $35 billion to $40 billion and growing.

Number three is, what is the industry growth rate? (Preferably stated in a three-year run rate.) The restaurant industry is a six to seven percent grower as a whole in the United States—why do you think McDonald's has been expanding so much in other countries?

By the way, half of this growth is simply through menu price increases, so real "organic" growth is actually 3 to 4 percent. That's why a company like California Pizza Kitchen (CPKI) is so exciting. The company has a three-year growth rate of 25 to 30 percent, which means it's taking market share. Therefore, I'm most interested in buying CPKI before Wendy's or McDonald's, whose mission is to maintain share and then hopefully grow.

CPKI is not encumbered with underperforming stores, ever-shifting menus and mediocre management. It is dynamic, passionate and laser-beam focused. It's a team you want to ride with. For further updates, go to www.stoplosingmoney-today.com.

## *Valuations and Variables*

The fourth point is where emotional detachment is critical: what is the current valuation of the individual company and the average valuation of the industry or the sector of the industry?

Valuation is looked at in a number of ways. The first is the probably the most quoted by brokers: what is the price- earnings ratio (PE) for this calendar year and next year? (This is the price divided by the earnings.) The rule of thumb is that one percent growth point normally equals one PE point.

For example, if a company has a three-year expected growth rate of 25 percent, the valuation can support a 20 to 30 times PE, mid-range being 25 times. California Pizza Kitchen, at this writing, has a 28 PE on 2006 earnings expectations and a "forward multiple" of 22 times expected 2007 earnings.

A superior grower like Google, with a nearly triple-digit revenue and earnings growth, can support a very high PE. Currently, GOOG 2006 PE is 44 times, and 2007 PE is 32 times; some say that although the PE is high, the stock is still cheap!

Obviously, one wants to buy stock from a company for which the PE is at a discount to its growth rate, or where the growth rate is understated and can expand.

The variables to the one point PE per one point per growth rate are more subjective. Does the Street like this management team? Remember, we are only human. We prefer nice, effective people who of course execute on their stated plans and communicate very well and clearly with the Street.

Another important variable: how visible are the revenues and earnings? Go back to Opsware, who opened their doors for business on January 1, 2006 with almost 60 percent of its revenues visible and accounted for. This gave comfort to investors.

The reason is that the OPSW business model recognizes the revenues ratably over the life of the contract, even if most of the contract has been paid up front. OPSW should have approximately 65 to 70 percent of its 2007 revenues visible on January 1, 2007.

Another variable is, how large is the company's installed base of (hopefully loyal) customers? For example, when Medtronic (MDT) launches a new cardiac pacemaker or implantable defibrillator, it has a ready audience of over 2,000 hospitals in the United States. These hospitals are already Medtronic customers, so their sales cycle and process becomes fairly short and predictable, unlike a new medical device company that may spend three months just to get invited in for a demonstration.

More variables: Has the company delivered the last three to six quarterly expectations consistent with analysts' published models? No one likes to be surprised, especially negatively. If a company has a history of hitting expectations, managing those expectations (go back to CFO!) and communicating clearly and quickly with the Street, investors sleep better at night.

## *Exceptions to the Rules*

Overall, if a company has a respected, mature management team; a large, addressable market or one that "it owns" (like SNPS); is recognized as "the" leader or the up-and-coming leader in its sector; and has a PE that is not out of whack with the three-year growth rate, bingo! Stock is a buy.

Man, isn't that simple? No. Because there are always exceptions and this is an imperfect world. What if the company has no earnings this year and probably next year as well?

We can look to several biotechnology companies for examples. The biotech world is event and announcement- driven. Also critical is which giant pharmaceutical company is aligned with which biotech company. The trend has been for giant pharmaceutical companies like Merck (MRK), Eli Lilly (LLY) and Schering-Plough (SGP) to spend less on their research and development and "outsource" it to focused biotech companies.

They then pay huge sums of money to these partners as they achieve certain "milestones" such as US Food and Drug Administration (FDA) approval to advance from phase one clinical trials to phase two clinicals. And, by the way, that is the precise moment you want to buy that biotech company.

Phase one is where most of the failures occur. Phase two is a beautiful time because the biotech company is receiving huge payments from its pharmaceutical partner, thus giving it much-needed operating cash, and its stock tends to really run up. The riskiest part of the story is now behind them. Phase two certainly carries its share of risk, but nowhere near that associated with phase one.

Phase three is even better, as more milestone payments come in and the biotech firm is really focused on getting its final FDA approval. But the money in the stock has been made in phase two. Take Advanced Magnetics (AVM), whose shares nearly tripled in 2005 on phase one data, FDA approval of that data and FDA permission to advance to phase two. So, the stock started moving up at the end of phase one and the money was made at the end of phase two.

As an aside, the biotech world can be confusing and very technical in its scientific terminology. Make absolutely sure your broker/adviser has access to a top-notch biotech analyst who has a scientific or in-industry background—preferably both. Someone from the Master of Business Administration (MBA) path with no scientific background will not last long as a biotech analyst!

Other examples of companies with no current earnings are those that are in the "investment mode." Emerging software companies typically have minimal to no earnings, such as Opsware (OPSW) and Salesforce.com (CRM). (Salesforce.com is in the customer relationship manager field—CRM—hence its stock symbol.) Both are just beginning to enter profitability.

During the past three years, both OPSW and CRM have had very high sales and marketing expenses, around 50 to 55 percent of revenues. These companies have needed to hire and retain top-notch salespeople and pay them competitively, as they have been seeding the market. Also, both have spent more than normal in the research and development area, as they needed to assure their customers, who are new, that their products are indeed superior.

So with no current earnings to gauge by, why are these two stocks a buy? Because they are both not only beginning to dominate their spaces, but they have also invented (OPSW) or reinvented (CRM) their respective spaces, which have been dominated in the past by Siebel Systems, acquired by Oracle.

Whereas Siebel would install a multimillion-dollar software system for its customers that would take months to deploy and train users on, Salesforce.com is a "hosted" model, very inexpensive per user, and all the data is transmitted over the Internet rather than tying up company database assets.

Salesforce.com is revolutionizing the software world. A stock to own—and for a long time. Also, both Opsware and Salesforce.com are competing in huge addressable markets, which investors reward with a bit higher valuation parameters.

## *What About the Earnings?*

As Opsware and Salesforce.com begin to have mass adoption by customers, the sales and marketing expenses will drop to a more normalized 25 to 28 percent, and research and development costs will fall as well, thus giving a huge leverage to the earnings (profits). Over three to five years, both companies will see their earnings as a percentage of sales in the 25 to 30 percent range, possibly even a bit higher.

Highly profitable businesses will command the higher PE multiples, especially if those profits are growing. Now, to be precise, some companies virtually "print money," meaning their operating margins (the profit before taxes) are quite high but their "top line" growth, or revenue growth, is fairly stagnant.

Three fairly well known companies in this camp are Microsoft (MSFT), Oracle Systems (ORCL) and Cisco Systems (CSCO). All three produce the "envy of the Street" operating margins in the 35 to 40 percent range. But in the past three years, the top line has barely managed 8 to 10 percent growth.

Microsoft, Oracle and Cisco are all at the top of their games, leaders in their respective fields, but they are currently not growth stocks. In fact, I'll share a little secret: professional portfolio managers wanted to jokingly hold a funeral service for Microsoft when it announced the one-time $3 per share dividend and initiated a quarterly dividend in 2004. The message from Microsoft was, "We cannot deploy these dollars to grow our business," so the dividend was declared. The shares have performed poorly ever since.

Another important piece of data to consider before buying a stock is, what is the PEG ratio? The PEG is price-earnings-to-growth ratio. This is figured by dividing the PE by the growth percentage.

Example: a company is trading at a 15 PE and the current

year's expected earnings growth rate (from the previous year) is 15 percent; therefore, the PEG is 1. A company trading at a 15 PE and earnings growth is expected at 10    percent, the PEG is 1.5 times.

Conversely—and more attractive because it's trading at a discount—is a company trading at a 10 PE and its expected growth rate is 15 percent, which equals a PEG of 0.67 times. At this writing, the PEG ratio for the entire S&P 500 is 1.22. This data is derived by looking at the earnings growth rate of the S&P 500 for 2006, which is currently 12.4 percent, and the average PE rate for the S&P 500, which is 15.18 times.

Typically, companies that have higher expected growth rates than the S&P growth rate will or should command a higher PEG ratio. Conversely, companies growing their earnings slower than the S&P growth rate will or should have a lower PEG ratio.

Some examples of current 2006 PEGs are the fast-growing software company Salesforce.com (CRM), with a PEG of 1.63; VeriSign (VRSN), with a PEG of 1.67; Medtronic (MDT), with a current PEG of 1.32; and Dow Chemical (DOW), with a PEG of 1.02.

In your decision process to buy a stock, the PEG ratio is an important number because the higher the PEG, the higher the expectations. One of the first questions a professional money manager will ask is, "What is the PEG?" Next he will want to know what the three to five-year expected growth rate of the company is and if they've been consistent the last three to six quarters.

As an aside, don't get hung up on or puzzled by the ratios, as they can get a bit confusing. Just know that a PEG above the S&P 500 average means good-to-great things are expected from the company. A PEG below the S&P 500 average indicates low expectations, recent or expected disappointments and a company out of favor. Sometimes "value" can be found in those companies, but the dynamics are very different from those of a growth company.

## *Putting the Numbers Together*

Here is an example of where the PEG ratio of the company, the S&P 500 five-year growth rate and the individual company's three to five-year growth rate do not match up—making the stock a buy!

First, a quick review. For 2006, S&P earnings growth rate is 12.4 percent. S&P 500 current PEG is at 1.22 for 2006 (remember, S&P average PE is 15.18, which divided by the 12.4 percent growth rate equals 1.22). But the five-year outlook is S&P growth at 10.55 percent, so the five-year PEG is currently at 1.44 (current PE at 15.18 times divided by five-year growth rate of 10.55 percent, which equals 1.44).

But enough of the mathematics lesson. Enter Progressive Gaming Corp. (PGIC).

PGIC has innovative technology for the gaming and casino industry, which is very highly regulated. Its technology allows, for example, a slot machine to be replaced by a "dumb terminal" through which a central server programs which game or theme goes into the slot machine, and can change it within minutes to a different theme or game. However, it will not change or mess with the odds.

Most slot machines cost $10,000 to $12,000 each, and they require costly maintenance at least three times per year. Dumb terminals, on the other hand, cost about $1,000 each and maintenance is minimal.

PGIC also has cutting-edge technology for the blackjack tables. It has developed an RFID—radio frequency identification device—that can actually be embedded into betting chips so that casinos can monitor and analyze betting behaviors and patterns. All of the company's technology is patented (always a good sign and also a good question to ask).

PGIC used to be a computer hardware company with terrible margins and high capital costs, but under new management in the past two and a half years, it's been retooled as a pure software play, with very high and growing margins.

New management has also been paying off and restructuring a heavy debt load that the company inherited. Debt has been cut in half (again, a good sign for earnings growth and acceleration), and the remaining debt will be eliminated in the next 12 months.

The transition to the "new business model" has had its painful moments. These growing pains have caused 2006 earnings guidance to be reduced. Nonetheless, the opportunity in front of this company is staggering. 2006 expected numbers are revenues of $93 million and earnings per share (EPS) of $0.20; 2007 expectations are revenues of $116 million and EPS of $0.52.

From a PE perspective, Progressive Gaming is at 50 times 2006 expected earnings, with a PE of 19 times 2007 expectations. The 2006 PEG is 1.2 times, and the exciting part is in 2007, when the PEG is 0.7 times! This is a compelling buy, just based on the numbers analysis alone.

But there are other intangibles present here. One, the gaming industry is highly regulated, so the barriers to entry are very high, keeping the competition down. PGIC has crossed the barriers: each state commission must approve every vendor that a casino buys from. This approval process requires a lot of time and money.

The other important intangible for PGIC is the recurring revenues. Each blackjack table that employs the RFID system must pay a daily user rate, after the initial large technology purchase. Talk about margins! This provides investors with that magical word: visibility. A company will fetch a higher PE multiple when investors see a good portion of their revenues are present for "just turning on the lights."

## *Revisions and Comparisons*

So why is PGIC so cheap, with a 2007 PEG of 0.7? Because of the downward earnings revision for 2006 and the shifting business model, which carries its own sets of risks, the company is in the "show me" stage. It's like potential investors are saying, "I hear your plan and it's terrific, but you had some early execution issues, so I'm putting you in the penalty box."

The way out of the penalty box is to execute the stated public expectations, implement your technologies around the world and don't revise anymore to the downside. All upside revisions, of course, are welcomed.

What makes it so attractive is the previous bad news and revisions are in the price already, hence a PEG of 0.7. My downside risk here is minimal and my upside is huge.

Analysts and PGIC management have endorsed a three to five-year earnings growth rate of 40 percent. As they begin to report the March quarter, then the June quarter, and numbers come in line or better, PGIC can easily command a 40 PE on 2007 earnings expectations of $0.52. So I would put the initial price target at $18, and the stock is currently $10.30. All they have to do now is execute!

Why an $18 price target, when the data and the market could easily support $20? The idea is to always have a price target on any stock you own. Setting a price target should discipline the investor to review the company with her broker as the stock approaches the target.

If, for example, PGIC hit $18, it would cause me to discuss with my broker the current fundamentals, any changes to the story, and so on. It does not necessarily mean I sell it; the target just gives me a hard reminder to validate and justify keeping, or not keeping, the stock.

The price target can easily be adjusted to a higher level. If PGIC in early 2007 is on track for $0.52 EPS, and by then 2008 earnings estimates would be published, say, at $0.70, I could move my price target up to $26 to $28.

If I perceive a slight slowdown in the growth rate—say 40 percent begins to look more like 30 percent—I will adjust my target to $22 to $23. But remember, as the stock approaches the initial target of $18, the thinking and reviewing process begins.

As an aside, I have been asked many times, "Where can an individual investor find important financial information about a company or how a company compares with its peer group?"

One of the best sources for up-to-date information—and it's free—is Yahoo.com. Once there, click on "Finance" and put a stock symbol in the quote space. After that search result appears, the left-hand column has several tabs for more information.

An example: to find the PEG ratio for an individual company, its peer group and the S&P 500, click on the "Analyst Estimates" tab, and all the information will be at your fingertips!

Choosing what to buy and buying the stocks is fun. Knowing when to sell or when to buy more is also fun but it can be gut wrenching—and a bit more emotional. But remember, removing emotions is a bit easier said than done. The next two chapters will discuss these dilemmas.

Stop losing money today…know when to buy!

## CHAPTER 6

## KNOWING WHEN TO SELL

WHEN DO YOU SELL A STOCK that had either given you a joyful profit—or a painful loss?

When to sell has given me the most profound insight into the human condition over the years. I have seen investors—both individual and professional portfolio managers—literally tear up upon selling a stock, as if it were a child leaving the nest. Notice I didn't say whether the selling was at a profit or a loss!

Although, I have seen investors selling at a loss treating the event like a death in the family. Remember, these are companies, not our children. But the idea is to stop losing money!

### *The Joy of It All*

So when do you sell a stock? Let's start with the happier event—selling at a profit.

Go back to the Progressive Gaming (PGIC) example. You bought the stock at $10 in April 2006, with the expectation that it would be $20, hopefully, in 12 months. If by October 2006 the shares are at $14, you will have already heard the June and September quarterly results.

If all is well and the results are in line, "steady as she goes"—no reason to sell a share. Let's say the overall market has also been steady. Great. No reason to sell. Let's say the overall market has been terrible. Still no problem. Remember, you own PGIC, not the market. Even though the general market may be holding it down a bit, that's still not a reason to sell. It may be a reason to buy more (which I'll discuss in the next chapter).

Fast forward to February 2007. The December 2006 quarter has come in better than expected, causing analysts to raise 2007 numbers from revenues of $116 million to $125 million, and earnings per share from $0.52 to $0.60. The stock is trading at $18 to $19 a share. Everything is great.

The ship is now really steady and picking up speed. As an investor, you are happy, but the stock is at your initial price target of $18. With the previously mentioned joyful events for PGIC, simply raise your price target. It is that simple, because the fundamentals and underlying numbers justify it.

With a new EPS of $0.60 for 2007—plus, analysts would have initiated their 2008 earnings estimates by then for, let's say, $0.80—move your price target up to $26 to $28 and go about your business. No reason to sell a share. I wish it were always this easy and smooth…sometimes it is!

## *Dealing With the Pain*

Sometimes, there will be less pleasant experiences. For example, let's say PGIC is up to $17, which is a nice move from $10, but the September quarter was "just okay."

The company, as we say, "limped across the finish line," barely making the September quarterly results. Management was a bit tepid about the expected December quarter, stating on the quarterly conference call that they were "comfortable with the low- to mid-end of the range."

(Important to note, not all analysts have the exact same revenue and earnings expectations. Estimates can range between 1 and 10 percent of each other; therefore, the average number is considered a "consensus.")

At this juncture you must review and justify your price target. The company has just given you a signal that either growth is slowing down or it has internal execution issues. You may really like (remember, we don't love) the PGIC story and may have planned to hold it for two to three years.

That's fine, but the $17 price may be $15 in a few weeks because of the "lack of enthusiasm." Sell some—maybe one-quarter to one-half of your total position—or the ultimate number of shares you plan to own. If you own 1,000, let go of 250 to 500. Lock in the profit.

If the shares do trade back to the $14 to $15 level, you can revisit and buy back (more on this in the next chapter).

Now for the bad-news scenario. PGIC has just missed, blown, torched, and—every trading desk's favorite expression—"puked" the December quarter. It missed both revenues and earnings expectations by 15 to 25 percent, and significantly reduced 2007 revenue guidance (expectations) from $116 million of revenues to $102 million, earning $0.52 to $0.30 per share.

If the stock was trading at $17 before the news became public, don't worry about gently selling the shares at $15 or $14, because they will already be at $12 in a heartbeat! Wall Street trading desks have a way of "marking 'em down" to the fair value in seconds!

So now you are angry, disappointed and frustrated. But take a deep breath and think about it. Should you sell your shares or just hold on for dear life?

## *Keep Yourself Informed!*

Here is a set of simple questions to ask your broker and analyst. Quite often the analyst's written update will contain at least his or her answers to most of them.

First question: has there been any specific slowdown in the industry, or is this "miss" in earnings and revenue guidance company-specific? How have PGIC's competitors done this past quarter—IGT Corp. and Shuffle Master being the two biggest?

If the industry growth rate is slowing, almost all the companies in the sector will eventually be marked down. Example: from mid-2001 to mid-2003, we saw the software sector growth rate implode. With that, all the valuations came down as well, whether it was Microsoft or a new start-up.

Another example: when the price of oil slowly fell from $20 per barrel to about $10 to $11 in 1997-1998, all energy stock valuations came down as well, from Exxon to the smallest West Texas driller. Misery loves company.

If it is an industry trend, then sell all your holdings in the sector. They will invariably have a comeback, but if it might take one to three years, why hold the shares? The sector becomes affectionately known in the portfolio management world as "dead money." But eventually all sectors have their resurrections, where "value" becomes growth again (more on this in a later chapter).

If the quarterly earnings miss is company-specific, more and different questions need to be asked. When did management realize the quarter was going to be missed? Was it midway through or in the last two days of the quarter?

These factors are important because they tell you the ratability, or evenness, of the business. Have past quarters been even-keeled throughout the 12 weeks, or are they normally back-end weighted? If they are normally even, then management knew (or should have known) early enough to "warn" the Street. If they are normally back-end weighted, then management really wouldn't know until very late in the quarter, or even until the quarter is finished.

Example: most computer hardware and software companies do 50 percent of their quarterly revenues the last two weeks of the quarter, sometimes even in the last two to three days. It can be nail biting. Their customers know that it's all back-end weighted; therefore, they try to drive their best bargains in the last week of the quarter.

On the other hand, the restaurant industry, medical device companies, pharmaceutical companies and the like tend to have ratability throughout the quarter.

As a funny aside, it's music to a portfolio manager's ears to know that a technology company CFO is on vacation the first week of the new quarter because that means the company has made the quarter that just ended!

## How Will the Company Recover?

But back to our disaster. Obviously, with a blown quarter, the revenue and earnings bar must be reset for the ensuing one to five quarters both by the analysts and by the company's CFO. It is almost a rule of thumb in the investing business: there is no such thing as one bad quarter or, to put it more bluntly, rarely is there only one cockroach in the kitchen!

The stock you own is already down due to the missed quarter; the Wall Street trading desks made sure of that. Now comes the trickier part: has the bar been reset low enough to avoid further bad news, or does it have to come down again in three months? Chances are the latter, so sell!

Also, in the past two to three years, CFOs have been reluctant to "bless" a new earnings and revenue number going forward, or they give a very wide range to the estimate. They are not being deceptive to the Street, but they just don't want to get burned—or burn the Street again. But it is a signal that there is more bad news to come. Lick your wounds and sell.

Growth companies do encounter growth pains along the way. Remember PGIC? I liked the story a great deal, but I got involved after they had encountered their difficulties and reset the bar twice. But I came to the story with a fresh set of eyes, without having suffered the pain others had endured earlier. Because PGIC had the "discounted" PEG, much of the downside risk had been eliminated. Not all, but most.

Another important question to ask is, if the operating margins have been driven down due to the missed quarter and the reduction of the forward guidance, can the company recover to normalized levels?

This is critical because operating margins do not lie! Everything above the operating margin line is expenses, such as cost of goods sold, labor, and research and development. So does my blown-quarter company need to invest more in sales and marketing? Or should they invest more in research and development? Or in bricks and mortar and inside infrastructure spending?

If normal operating margins were at 12 percent, for example, but going forward we could expect them to settle in at 9 to 10 percent—I've heard this before!—then the valuation, or stock market value of the company, even when it recovers, will not be the same. It will not command the same PE even when times improve. That's the time to sell!

Quick example: Microsoft has current operating margins of 39 to 40 percent—obscenely high, but they were actually in the mid-40s earlier in the decade. So as powerful as those operating margins are, even though they're the envy of about 5,000 other companies, they still have come down and the valuation has not been the same since.

## *Integrity Equals Profits*

Another issue that causes investors to "shoot first and ask questions later" is the credibility of management. I have seen companies address an audience of portfolio managers on a Tuesday at a growth conference, saying all is well and that they're "tracking to Street estimates."

Then, they turned around and pre-announced a shortfall in revenues and profits on Friday, at 5:30 p.m. Eastern time, hoping no one would catch it! This was not good. It could take a year or longer for credibility to be built back up—if it ever was. Until then, the stock would carry a discounted PE multiple.

Investors would have respected the company and its management more if they had canceled the growth stock conference appearance and gone straight to the pre-announcement, rather than showing up and playing "smoke and mirrors." They would have still crushed the stock, but recovery would have been much quicker as "investor confidence" would not have totally disappeared.

The issue was that no one was sure if management lied or if they had no real idea that the quarter was going poorly. Either way, it was not good.

However, Wall Street does have a way of forgiving those who 'fess up. Case in point—a firm whose CEO has just retired. Interwoven (IWOV), a Silicon Valley software company, has excellent, respected technology. Their products provide enterprise content management for customers and the customers' end users; it's quite complicated, yet critical for those who create complex documents and need to share them.

The CEO was there for the IPO back in 1996, made a fortune, retired in 2001, came back in 2003 to "salvage" the company, then re-retired for good in early 2006. He was the most ego-driven CEO I have ever encountered. He was extremely promotional despite the fact that investors just want the facts, not a commercial and he didn't always have command of the company's numbers.

In late 1999, IWOV missed a quarter—not badly, but the growth rate was so strong and yet they still missed. I happened to be out visiting with four British portfolio managers. The CEO kept stressing how they could become heroes by buying the stock right then.

I nearly killed him on the spot. The portfolio managers were polite, as the British normally are, and then proceeded to sell every share they owned. The CEO had destroyed his credibility.

IWOV has been interesting these past two years. By every measurement, the stock is dirt cheap, but as long as that CEO was involved, most professional money managers would not touch the story. Maybe with his retirement, IWOV is worth re-examining.

The tougher question to answer comes down to a gut feeling: what should I do if my stock has done well over the last year or two, but it's just languishing around now at these levels?

It's interesting because there is no bad news to analyze or bar to reset. The stock isn't flourishing simply because there isn't any real new money going into it, and no real money is coming out, either. In other words, as we say, "the stock is trading sideways." I saw this with DuPont (DD) in 2001 to 2004, when their stock traded in a narrow range. The company did not disappoint in earnings or revenues—it was just boring.

This selling decision comes down to a gut feeling about whether you can better deploy these dollars elsewhere. This can also happen when a stock performs really well. Sometimes it hits the price target and there is no real fundamental reason to sell, but your gut feeling is that the stock will just "rest" there for a while. It's a nice problem to have!

## *Dishonesty Is Not the Best Policy*

One issue that raises no "buy or sell" questions is the matter of a company's management lying outright or clearly being deceptive. It may not be illegal, but it's certainly unethical.

Also, if a major lawsuit—not a nuisance suit—is filed against the company claiming some serious charges or damages, sell no matter what; there will only be more pain to come. This is a case of "shoot first, then shoot again!" I learned this one very painfully. Here's the quick story…

In the mid-90s, the electronic design automation (EDA) sector was dominated by two companies, Synopsys (SNPS) and Cadence Design (CDN). But a new player was emerging and making a lot of noise and inroads: Avant! (AVNT).

By the way, the first red flag here should have been the exclamation point. It was included in the true, legal spelling of the company name: Avant!

The company was winning some major semiconductor contracts in the United States and Asia, taking business away from Cadence and even Synopsys. The Avant! CEO, Gerry Hsu, had been at Cadence for 10 years and then left to form Avant! with what he thought was a better mousetrap.

Gerry was energetic, dynamic and focused like a laser beam; in short, as portfolio managers had aptly labeled him, he was an animal. He loved meeting investors, told great war stories and really enjoyed publicly kicking Cadence around (another red flag, in hindsight). Avant! stock was a rocket ship; numbers were coming in above expectations, quarter after quarter. All was terrific—and then, boom!

Cadence Design filed a major lawsuit against Avant!, claiming they had stolen 4,000 out of 1.4 million lines of code for its new software product. That's where the war began.

Cadence was able to secure a temporary injunction against Avant!, which Avant! was able to get overturned, claiming customers would be hurt too much by "this nonsense." Customers—and we are talking names like Texas Instruments, Samsung and even Intel—were indeed nervous, because the new EDA software was critical to their new chip designs.

Avant! went on the warpath, claiming Cadence was just jealous because it was losing market share and its own engineers to the newer company, which was accurate. But every time anyone asked Gerry Hsu if the charges were true, all we ever got was general mumbo jumbo—another red flag.

Gerry even went so far as to hire a bodyguard, as he claimed he was being followed. What a soap opera. Avant! stock really bounced around because during this period, it still hit Wall Street numbers—even exceeded them—and the company's software was indeed critical for its customers.

Of course, I was in my naïve, "I love the company" phase then so I defended Gerry, traveled with him to see clients and really got behind him. I finally woke up one day and thought, sanely and finally, Do I really know if Gerry is telling the truth?

I did not have enough technical knowledge about EDA software code, but I did know that Avant! recruited several Cadence engineers in the past two years. Who knows, maybe one of them brought the code with him. I mean, who would look for 4,000 lines among 1.4 million lines of code? Stop this train…I'm getting off.

## Know When to Sell

I told all my clients about my "awakening" and fortunately, they all sold before it really hit the fan. Avant! was found guilty, Gerry is somewhere in Taiwan and has not been seen in the United States for the last seven years and Synopsys bought out what was left of Avant!—and dropped that darn exclamation point.

69

I should explain that if you own stock mutual funds, whether aggressive growth, simple growth or growth and income funds, the time to buy is always. Mutual funds take a bit of the guesswork and fun out of investing, but millions of investors feel more comfortable with this approach. (We'll discuss mutual funds more in a few chapters.)

One strategy is to have one-third to one-half of your investible funds in mutual funds and the rest in individual stocks. Well, whatever makes you tick, do not ignore individual stocks—that's where the financial adventures lie.

Stop losing money today. Know when to sell!

## CHAPTER 7

## KNOWING WHEN TO BUY MORE

LET'S EXPLORE THE MYSTERY of when to buy more. One of the biggest mistakes made by individual investors is to buy their "full position" of a stock all at once. Your broker/adviser calls you with a well thought out, well-researched idea, you ask all the appropriate questions discussed in the "Trust…but Verify" chapter and you mutually agree to buy the stock. Chances are, you buy your whole position right on the spot.

Wrong! Professional portfolio managers rarely, if ever, buy their whole position at one time. They buy incrementally.

### *Practical Skepticism—And When to Ignore It*

A bit of explanation: the legendary British portfolio manager Dr. Michael Mullaney (remember BroadVision?) used to buy his stocks in increments. He would buy half his position to begin, as he would say, the "journey."

He'd follow the stock carefully and do more research and analysis. He would wait anywhere from a day to a year before filling out his final position. Michael had incredible patience, one of his great attributes.

If the stock moved up or down 10 percent, he would generally buy another one-quarter to one-third of his eventual final number. If the stock moved up another 10 percent, he'd finish buying the rest of the position. His reasoning was, "others are beginning to see what I see."

If the stock moved down another 10 percent, he would also finish buying the rest of his position, calmly saying, "I'm early!" His methodology was brilliant, calculating, almost formulaic—but a lot of his decisions were also just gut feelings. Michael had a sense of timing that I've never seen duplicated.

The idea here is that a stock may move with the general market, unrelated to the fundamentals of the story. If you buy Apple Computer (AAPL) at $58 and for whatever reasons, the general market takes it to $54, besides the $4, what has changed? If the answer is "nothing," add to it; buy more.

By the way, what if the opposite happens? If you own Apple at $58 and it moves to $62, what has changed? Again, if the answer is "nothing," add to it. Remember, you are an investor building a position. If you are a trader, someone who actively buys just to sell and is not in it for the long term, you might sell it at $62, thank you very much, and move on…but then you missed the move to $90!

Let's go back to the "I'm early; the rest of the pack will catch up soon" idea. You've bought a stock, you and your broker feel it may be a bit early for the story or the sector, but you are pretty confident. As the stock moves up in value, this sometimes serves as confirmation that the company is now "getting traction."

Example: brilliant Internet media analyst Stewart Barry of ThinkEquity Partners put a buy rating on aQuantive (AQNT) at $8 back in late 2004. AQNT, a Seattle-based Internet advertising/media company, had acquired a similar-sized company called Razorfish in early 2004. The two companies merged and needed some "digestion" time to see where the synergies were, the cost savings and so on.

At one point, Stewart felt that the digestion period was over, but more importantly, that Internet-based advertising was about to enter an incredible period of mega-growth. He felt quite confident in his thesis and recommended the shares of AQNT at $8.

Many clients were a bit skeptical, as they felt perhaps the merger pain of aQuantive and Razorfish might not be totally over yet and that another quarter or two of joint results would provide greater comfort. Not a totally unreasonable opinion, as investors do become temporarily skittish about a company if it has announced a large acquisition or merger. These things rarely go as smoothly as one hopes.

But a few brave souls began buying shares of aQuantive around the $8 to $9 level. As the company moved through the December quarter of 2004 and the March quarter of 2005, it became apparent that they were becoming the "go to" company and that any nervousness over merger issues were gone.

Stock started to lift to the $13, $14, $15 level, picking up in trading volume (which is important and will be discussed later) as investors were "piling in." I had one portfolio manager who bought a one-third position at the $8 to $9 level, and then really piled in at $15. This is why he missed a near double, as he only had one-third of the shares needed to fill out his position.

Yes, he did miss a near double, but the fundamentals and the risk profile (much less risk) were actually a lot stronger at $15 than at $8. So, he bought both: at $8, one-third position and at $15, the rest of his position. His average buy-in price was about $12.50.

The stock ran up to $30 in early 2006 and is now a verifiable "monster." My client did a bit of selling—half his shares around the $27 to $28 level—because he wanted to buy them back at the $22 to $23 level. Sure enough, aQuantive did trade back to $22 in April 2006, and he rebought his half position.

## *The Ups and the Downs*

Now why do all that work on a winning idea? Because stocks rarely go straight up (although sadly, some have gone straight down!). Stocks that go up like AQNT, from $8 to $30 per share, normally go up incrementally. Many times it's up $3 to $4, then down $1 to $2.

Why? Because there are active traders out there and hedge funds that play the 5 to 10 percent game: buy a stock, make or lose 5 to 10 percent and then get out. With AQNT, there was some solid profit taking as well. Remember, they nearly doubled from $8 to $15 before the story really went mainstream.

At nearly 100 percent profit, no one will criticize someone for selling; nor will anyone make a fuss over those who bought in the $14 to $15 level and sold at $28 to $30. Let's say you were lucky enough to have bought AQNT at $8 to $9 and it's now trading at $24 (at this writing)—should you buy more? They have the opportunity to be a very big story, a potential $9 billion to $10 billion market cap company (currently at $1.6 billion market cap). The answer is yes, I would buy more.

When would you not buy more? If it's at $24, you and your broker need to re-ask all the important fundamental questions and pretend you are looking at aQuantive for the first time (remember, no emotions; detach and be objective, even though the stock has tripled). How big is the addressable market and how is aQuantive positioned within it? Are they considered the leader? Where is the competition?

Further, you should ask if the company's pricing model—the method by which it set its products' prices—is holding up. If it's not, is it factored into the 2006-2007 earnings and revenue model? Where are the operating margins now and where are they going?

The answers may not be good enough to justify buying more shares here, or the answers may be, Wow! This story is just starting and the shares could double or triple again from here. Be objective: don't let the fact that your investment has doubled or tripled be "the" factor. As I mentioned, I would buy more AQNT because the sector is only in the first or second inning and they are the de facto standard.

## Surviving the Sector Rotations

Another scenario: my stock has done okay, but it seems to be drifting down for no apparent reason. It's just drifting, trading sideways in a narrow range. Do I buy more? What do I look for?

The first fact I want to know is what the average daily volume for the past three months has been. Volume-traded can reveal a lot. There may be no real negative news circulating about the company, but my stock may be "rotated out," as can be the sector itself.

Great. Now what? Industries tend to move in sync together, with the leaders outperforming the followers, but the rising tide will lift all boats. Conversely, the lowering tide will sink all boats.

Volume-traded can strongly indicate this phenomenon one way or the other. A 20 to 30 percent higher-than-normal volume trading in your stock or sector, say for two to three weeks, tells me money is moving in or out of the sector. For example, in 2005, pharmaceuticals were being rotated out, but the biotech sector was being rotated in.

The average volume for both sectors was higher than normal. In late 2004 and early 2005, the energy sector was being rotated in, in a huge way, with average volumes more than 30 to 40 percent above normal. In such a situation, if my stock is in the pharmaceutical space, what do I do? Buy more?

If the fundamentals are still intact and you have the patience, then buy more. Invariably, rotation back into pharmaceuticals will happen. When? I don't know, but it will. It always does. By the way, at this writing, the energy sector is currently being rotated out!

Rotation into and out of certain industries can last from six months to a year, but it should not be confused with an industry's or sector's fundamental shift.

In 2001, the software and hardware sectors began a two to three-year nuclear winter. The underlying fundamentals changed in a big way. The growth rates were coming down and, of course, so were the valuations, which were lofty and in some cases insane.

The fundamentals began to recover in early 2004, but the rotation in began in mid to late 2003. The volumes picked up and the money flow was moving back into the general technology space. The valuations were kept within reasonable limits for the companies that emerged from that disastrous period!

Remember, knowing when to buy more stock begins with re-analyzing all the fundamental questions you asked when you bought the stock in the first place. Remove any emotions and go about the work detached and objectively.

Stop losing money today…know when to buy more stock!

## CHAPTER 8

# IDENTIFYING GREAT COMPANIES—AN INSIDER'S INSIGHTS

IN MY MORE THAN A QUARTER CENTURY in the investment business, I have witnessed some phenomenal events in the stock market. I have had the opportunity to see great companies form, go through the initial public offering stage, have their growing pains, stay the course or right the ship, re-deploy their assets and finally thrive.

## *Discovering Your Company*

It always starts with great management teams—people with vision, character and perseverance. Examples could fill up five books, but some well-known success stories are Cisco Systems, Microsoft, Intuit, Monster.com, First Data Corp., Nike, Brinkers (Macaroni Grill and Chili's), Starbucks, Apple Computer and IBM (yes, IBM).

I have also seen many companies fall flat on their faces. They misinterpreted their market opportunities and their customer needs, mismanaged their precious financial assets, underinvested in research and development, had mediocre sales management and, worst of all—a cardinal sin—had bad senior management.

Remember how bad senior management missed their markets and caused companies like Montgomery Ward, Polaroid, Xerox, Kmart and Lone Star Steakhouse and Saloon to be worth less—or to disappear completely?

A quick note of differentiation here is important: insider insights versus inside information. Inside information is material information about a company that is not available to the general public, nor has it been announced by the company. It can be either good news or bad news but if it's acted upon, it could lead to criminal prosecution.

On the other hand, insider insights are not illegal. It is fun and challenging to determine what is occurring in the industry where a company plays, or what trends can be identified through observation and analysis.

So what is the magic, the secret sauce? How do you as an individual investor find and identify great current and up-and-coming companies? Not to be repetitive, but make sure you are really comfortable and communicative with your broker. Put your broker—whether it's a new relationship or an existing one—through the process we discussed back in chapter 2. An old dog can learn new tricks!

Also, it's okay to have two or even three brokers. No one individual or brokerage firm has a lock on the great ideas of this decade or the next (personally, I have three brokers, including myself). You may want to select a "national" firm such as Merrill Lynch, UBS Securities or Citigroup (the old Smith Barney) for more general research and for larger industry theme pieces.

But also look to the smaller regional firms like Legg Mason, Raymond James, AG Edwards, Piper Jaffray and Edward Jones for specialty growth research and for smaller to mid-cap names. These firms tend to specialize in regional companies, as they are sometimes much better equipped to find the stars of tomorrow, today.

Also, there is a very good chance that your broker can actually speak with and have a relationship with his analysts at the smaller regional firms. A Merrill Lynch broker will rarely, if ever, actually speak to an analyst. The firm is way too big for that kind of service, and it's layered with a lot of bureaucracy. In fact, "research liaison" people are common at a firm like Merrill Lynch; they interpret the analysts' daily notes and then regurgitate it back to the "retail force."

It is a very watered-down approach. But the smaller firms have much greater access for the broker, and sometimes the client can even speak to an analyst directly.

Research boutique firms like JMP Securities, Pacific Growth, Pacific Crest, Roth Capital and ThinkEquity Partners do not work with individual investors, but as I mentioned before, contact a research assistant and try to get on his or her email research distribution list.

## *Keep an Eye Out for the Innovators*

When you begin the search for great ideas to own, start with a series of questions (yes, again with the questions!). What sector looks interesting now and why? Is the sector cyclical or is it on a solid growth trajectory?

Examples: the biotechnology and medical device industries are on a growth trajectory. We have 77 million baby boomers, ages 42 to 60, and many will need new knees, hips and shoulders—ah, the aging athletes!—as well as cardiac devices such as pacemakers or implantable defibrillators.

There are many successful companies in cardiac care, like Medtronic (MDT), St. Jude Medical (STJ) and Eli Lilly (LLY). Yes, Lilly; it's a pharmaceutical company but getting bigger in cardiac care.

The orthopedic space has big winners as well, with Zimmer Holdings (ZMH), Biomet (BMT) and Stryker Corp. (SYK).

But there are also some smaller, emerging companies in these industries, like Intralase (ILSE) for eye care and Dexcom (DXCM), makers of an insulin pump, glucose-monitoring machine for the home treatment of diabetes.

Cyclical companies in industries such as heavy manufacturing, home building and automotive will have their times in the sun, but then sunset will arrive and you'll hope to be long gone. The trick is to catch them at dawn and certainly sell before dusk. (There will be more about cyclicals in the next chapter.) Examples here are Caterpillar, John Deere, Toll Brothers and Daimler Chrysler.

Another important question to ask is, who is leading the field? Leaders lead and followers follow. Medtronic and Zimmer Holdings are arguably the leaders in the major medical device field, Medtronic for cardiac and Zimmer for orthopedics. There are other fine companies in both fields, but these two stand out, at least for now.

So who is building the better mousetrap? Is there a young start-up that will knock one or both off their strides? I don't know, but I carefully watch the research and development dollars (R&D) these two spend.

R&D is the future of Medtronic and Zimmer Holdings, or any company that has newer, evolving technology within their field. If I see a deceleration or an acceleration in R&D spending, I want to know why. Medtronic has a consistent history of spending about 10 percent of its revenues on R&D, and Zimmer Holdings has consistently spent about 7 percent of its revenues on its R&D effort. As long as those numbers are consistent, I can sleep well.

The same goes for computer hardware and software, pharmaceuticals (although much is outsourced to biotechs) and many other industries. R&D represents the future product-flow, so dollars spent there should not be scrimped on.

An insider insight: beware of a company that suddenly lowers its R&D spending, as it may be cutting there to achieve near-term earnings estimates. A good question to ask your broker is, what products are being developed in the company's R&D program? For competitive reasons, many companies are quiet about their "pipelines," but it's worth asking if there's an effort to enhance the current products or if it's a brand-new line up.

Medtronic is always working on the next pacemaker, to keep up with St. Jude Medical. But if they're working on a spinal product or a cardiac surgical product, this information can be invaluable because it can potentially expand the company's product line and its revenue opportunities. It never hurts to ask! The new upstart here can sometimes sneak up and hurt a dominant company like Medtronic or Zimmer.

The same concept of consistent spending as a percentage of sales does not apply to the selling, general and administrative expenses (SG&A). Other than the cost of goods sold and R&D, SG&A represents most of the other costs to run a business.

You want this percentage to fall as a business scales or rises—that is where the leverage is. Scale and leverage never come out of the R&D line. Selling and general expenses can vary a bit from quarter to quarter and begin a rising tide; however, the revenue should rise even more proportionally to account for rising SG&A.

This is how and where the operating margin begins to "scale." The operating margin is what's left after all expenses are tallied up before taxes and for definitional reasons, the net margin is the after-tax number. But the operating margin is the key to any story. As I mentioned before, it never lies. It is the true barometer of where a company is in its life cycle or development.

The insider's insight here is: if SG&A does go up as a percentage of total sales for more than a quarter or two, this is a red flag. Is the company "buying" its customers? Are they overspending on advertising or raising sales commissions to incent key salespeople?

It's a red flag, but not necessarily a disaster. If it does occur for a quarter or two, it may be because of a new product launch or the expense of hiring and training key sales and marketing people for anticipated growth. There is a "train up" period before salespeople or a new major product or campaign becomes productive and hopefully drives higher profitability.

If it happens for more than two consecutive quarters, however, questions must be answered. This was a red flag for Cisco Systems in late 2001. SG&A was up four quarters in a row, as they were trying to maintain their costly infrastructure, but revenues were not keeping pace; thus, the percentage for SG&A went up and stayed up, and the company began to lower future earnings guidance.

The key here is, you do not have to be an accountant and don't get all caught up in minutiae. Just be aware—and make sure your broker is as well—of the general ranges of these numbers and percentages. Just as you have a price target for your stock, all public companies have a "target" for their operating margins.

## Fads or Phenomena?

The fun part of analyzing companies is identifying which category their idea fits in. Is it a fad, a phenomenon or a niche? The iPod from Apple (AAPL) is a phenomenon because still only one in seven consumers owns one; older iPods are already being replaced by newer, better models and the services available for it are just beginning.

Today's $90 blue jeans by hot designer True Religion (TRLG) are a fad because they may be replaced by another style by next season. TRLG may sustain for a while, but do I want to put investment dollars there for three, four or five years? Probably not, but it could be great fun for a year or so.

Remember L.A.Gear? Hotter than a pistol for a couple of years, and then they just cratered as they "missed" the fashion shift. Ouch!

I have another example where the fad worked and then faded, but the underlying fundamentals continue to be a phenomenon. About a year and a half ago, in September 2004, I asked Stratton Sclavos, CEO of VeriSign (VRSN), if cell phone "ringtones" were a fad or a phenomenon. He was honest and said he wasn't sure.

Here's the quick story. In early 2004, VeriSign acquired a German company called Jamba for $273 million. Jamba basically distributed ringtones to cell phone owners through the major telecom companies. Jamba charged customers by the ringtone, or they could pay a monthly subscription fee for unlimited ringtones.

Now in 2002 through 2004, ringtones were huge in Europe and the United Kingdom; they were a good one-and-a-half to two years ahead of the United States. Kids were downloading ringtones like crazy (hence why I asked Stratton if it was only a fad), swapping them, changing them and so on.

In fact, the number one song in the United Kingdom in 2005 was the "Crazy Frog" ringtone, which was actually the theme song from Eddie Murphy's Beverly Hills Cop movie. It drove adults in the UK absolutely nuts!

In September 2004, four clients and I were having dinner with Stratton—of course, we were all emotionally detached, however—and we asked him about Jamba. His eyes lit up and we knew right away that the Jamba unit of VeriSign was really hot. Stock was trading at $18.

We discussed the fad versus the phenomenon concept, but we all concluded that no matter what the answer was, the next two to three quarters looked beautiful. The stock was a table-pounding buy!

Sure enough, the September 2004 quarter and the ensuing December quarter were better than expected, and VeriSign literally doubled to $36 by March 2005. But that question still pestered me: was it still just a fad?

Hardly anyone was paying attention to the rest of VeriSign's fundamental, core business: the website digital security certificates and the registrations of .com and .net. Instead, everyone was focused on the darned ringtone business, especially since the they were now available to US customers.

Listening to VeriSign's conference call for its March 2005 quarterly results (which by the way was open to all investors), I heard one sentence that grabbed me: "We don't know yet if there is any seasonality in the ringtone business." Boom! Goodbye!

I love—I mean, I like Stratton, but if he didn't know about any seasonality yet, that scared me. I told this to all my clients and fortunately they all sold their VeriSign shares between $32 and $35. We saw VeriSign trade back down to the $19 to $20 level as indeed there was "seasonality" in the June and September 2005 quarters. The earnings bar was reset in October 2005, and VeriSign became a table-pounding buy again at $19.

## The Moral of the Story

What's the insider's insight here? With the Apple iPod, we know that the November and December sales will be much larger than the January and February sales due to heavy Christmas gift buying. In fact, Apple sold 14 million iPods in the fourth quarter of 2005 and 8.5 million in the first quarter of 2006.

In general, we know that the fourth quarter of the year is bigger than the first quarter for most retailers. The same goes for technology companies due to "budget flush." Any government agency, school system and most corporations will "spend" their budgets in the fourth quarter. It's use it or lose it! These factors are built into the financial models. They are understood and clearly communicated.

But when a company "isn't sure" or "doesn't know" if there is seasonality, a disaster could be looming. I could have been wrong here, as VeriSign could have gone on to have two or three more quarters of great ringtone growth, but the risk/reward profile had shifted dramatically. Also, since the stock had doubled in six months, any hint of anything negative would have lowered the stock price $5 to $15 off the high.

That is what happened, but back at $19 and expectations having been reset, the stock was a strong buy. The underlying core business, the "stuff that brought them to the party" was intact, growing very smoothly and sustainable. Any upside from there on in the ringtone business was pure gravy, but it was not the reason to buy and own as it was during "fad time."

## What Is a Niche Player?

A company makes a very good product, but the addressable market is limited. Or the company makes a very good product, but that's it. They're affectionately known as a "one-trick pony"—or a niche player.

Niche players usually have two roads on which to travel: be acquired or eventually fade away. A current niche player is Interwoven (IWOV), who are very good in the complex

85

content management space for software and web developers. It's a limited market in size and scope, and customers tend to be loyal.

However, the growth will be difficult to sustain over a longer period of time and frankly, Interwoven would be better off with either IBM, Oracle or Hewlett-Packard Compaq (HPQ) as its parent.

The table was set back in 2004, when the leading company in content management, Documentum, was acquired by EMC Corp. Interwoven is doing the right things at present to build and showcase its business—expanding its operating margins, controlling SG&A and spending wisely in R&D— but the company's sustainability is still in question.

Another example here of insider's insights that paid off very nicely for my clients is a company called Jamdat (not to be confused with VeriSign's Jamba).

Jamdat distributed games for cell phones. They did it very well, too—they had major telecom relationships and offered about 30 different cell phone games. It was a niche company for sure, and it was not going to sustain itself for the long term.

The key insight here is that this company spent minimally on R&D but spent lavishly on SG&A, developing telecom carrier relationships and heavily advertising its brand. They played their cards very well and were bought out at a hefty premium by giant Electronic Arts (ERTS).

This was brilliant move on the larger company's part, since it opened them up to the world of wireless content and Jamdat brought them the carrier relationships! This allowed Electronic Arts to step into that medium without having to invest enormous time and energy. Look for Madden 2007 in wireless!

## *Sometimes, It Can Be Both!*

One company that began as both a niche and a fad but has emerged as a continuing market leader phenomenon is Nike (NKE). Remember when they just made running shoes in the late 70s and early 80s? Jogging was just taking off and many viewed them as a short-term fad or a niche player.

Nike was and still is brilliant; they went on to include all types of shoes for virtually every sport. They also designed and marketed great athletic apparel and casual wear for men, women and children.

It is a marketing machine and has successfully opened many Niketown retail shops; it also distributes through other retail channels. It has controlled its brand from day one.

The same can be said about Apple Computer (AAPL) Opening their own stores was a brilliant move. But they've successfully marketed through many other retail channels like Circuit City and Best Buy, so why would they open their own stores?

Insider's insight here: if you go to Best Buy or Circuit City to buy an iPod or an Apple Macintosh computer, chances are you'll buy just what you came for, or maybe even get diverted to a different brand. At the Apple store, not only will you buy the iPod or the Mac, but the accessories, the traveling cases, and everything else to go with it.

In their own stores, Apple controls the entire purchase as well as all future maintenance and upgrades. The same is true with the Niketown stores: you go in wanting to buy a pair of shoes but will invariably buy Nike sweatsocks, t-shirts and warm-up gear, too. They offer all Nike products and are consistent with their quality; they've controlled the total purchase and their brand. Don't be surprised to see Dell go retail in the future!

The other insider's insight is that Apple and Nike know exactly who their customer is. They are not trying to be "all things to all people." Apple is not going to win in the corporate marketplace for computers. Businesses will continue to buy from Dell, IBM and Compaq.

Apple clearly wants to own the consumer market and the educational/student market. They do and will continue to own the iPod market. Remember, iPod is a "brand" name; the real technology is called the MP3 player, but like the public's use of Kimberly Clark's (KMB) "Kleenex" brand name when referring to facial tissues, the use of "iPod" has solidified the brand and has linked it with the actual product name.

## *Know the Heck Out of Your Customers*

Let's look now at two companies who go above and beyond when it comes to working their markets: TCF Corp (TCB) and Wells Fargo Bank (WFC).

TCF, formerly known as Twin Cities Federal, is a Minnesota-based bank. William Cooper (recently retired but still on the board of directors), a very capable CEO, was brought on in the early 90s to turn things around.

He quickly identified his core customer base. As Bill often stated, "It's Joe Lunch Bucket and the college students." And that was it, period. He marketed to that sector, serviced them extremely well. He put bank branches in several grocery store chains, making it easy to bank, extended their hours to match the grocery stores', offered free checking as the "capturing" product and actually put tellers in the branches to help customers through the maze of other TCF financial products and services.

In the states and cities where TCF operates, it owns its sector of the market. Bill Cooper identified the customers and serviced the heck out of them. The stock was a near ten- bagger in the past 13 years.

On the other side, Dick Kovacevich, CEO of Wells Fargo

Bank, headquartered in San Francisco, determined early in his reign who his customers were: middle-aged, upscale professionals and large and small businesses.

Dick realized early on that being a lender to the world's developing nations could bring in higher interest rates and therefore potentially higher returns, but also major headaches. Who do you talk to when a country defaults? So he kept Wells Fargo away from the international lending market and focused purely in the United States.

Wells Fargo does an amazing amount of work for its customers. Usually customers end up with at least three or four Wells Fargo products such as checking, savings, mortgages and retirement and college plans. As Dick has said, "We want to own them, never give them a reason to leave."

Both Bill Cooper and Dick Kovacevich have been very successful and consistent, and so has their respective stock performances. If I heard that Wells Fargo wanted to go after international markets or governments, I would look to sell the stock. If TCF, who does have some business accounts and mortgages, were to try to go "upscale," I would sell its stock as well. They both should and will likely stick to their knitting.

## *Form Your Own Insider's Insights*

Look carefully in your home or place of work. What's happening in each? What's new? Look at your kids' world: what 14-year-old doesn't own (or at least have access to) a cell phone, an iPod or a portable DVD player?

Do your kids IM (instant message) their friends? Have a homepage on Myspace.com? They do their homework on their own or the family's computer and know how to Google just about anything. Five or 10 years ago, it was rare to have a personal email address; now, if you don't, you're lost.

Insider's insight comes from many different areas. All companies have Websites that can help you better understand your investment. Take a look at these sites. Are they warm and inviting or difficult to navigate? Does it have a lot of information for an investor, such as new and current products, news on whether the company is hiring additional employees (always a good sign) and recent press releases?

Look at your car, your digital camera, your DVD player, your new HDTV (another big wave that is just beginning), your sporting goods, your new clothes, the new restaurants around town. Who makes these things? Who are the suppliers to these companies that make these things?

If the new restaurant is busy on a Friday night and it's a public company, great—but ask the waiter if they are busy on a Monday or Tuesday. Are they hiring to add to staff or just to replace them?

Retailers love to talk about their business. Are those new style jeans selling well?

Ask your doctor or nurse what's new in his or her world. New devices? New medicines? (Remember MELA?) You get the idea.

One way to sharpen your own insider's insights is to phone the headquarters of a company and ask for the investor relations (IR) department. Many individual investors have told me over the years that IR people would only speak to big shareholders, so why bother?

But that's absolutely false! IR people speak to everyone from million-share holders all the way to 50-share holders. That is their job and their function. They are just more accustomed to speaking to larger institutional shareholders because very few individual shareholders ever call!

That being said, you'd be surprised by the information that can be obtained from an IR representative. Not inside information, as that is illegal if acted upon, as we discussed earlier, but insider insights. Ask the IR person if the new product is selling well. Is it being well received in the marketplace? Are some geographies selling better than others? Is the pricing model holding up?

Furthermore, ask if the company is presenting at any growth conferences in the next three months. Can you view the presentation on the company's website? Can the IR person put you on his email list so you can receive company press releases? (This is important because you don't want to find out about the news, good or bad, three days after the fact.)

Smaller companies will sometimes have their VP of finance, or even the CFO, act as the IR representative. This is even better, because your information flow will be fresher and coming from an authority within the company.

## *My Picks*

Here are some of my great growth opportunities for 2006 and 2007, some of which were discussed earlier: Homestore (MOVE), Progressive Gaming Corp. (PGIC), Salesforce.com (CRM), aQuantive Corp (AQNT) and Apple Computer (AAPL).

Homestore is an aggregator on the Web of 2 million real estate listings across the country. Although 73 percent of all real estate inquiries, whether buy or sell, begin on the Web, only 3 to 4 percent of the advertising/marketing dollars are spent on the Web. This is changing, and Homestore is the potential gorilla in the space.

Progressive Gaming Corp. is a leading firm in the "back of the house" to the casino and gaming industry. With very high barriers to entry, PGIC is positioned for the slot machine change to a "dumb terminal" with the functions centralized on a central server. This allows casinos to switch games on the fly.

Also, PGIC has a patented radio frequency identification system (RFID). These chips track information at the gaming tables, allowing casinos to monitor when and how much is bet at a time. These "intelligent" tables and the ability to change games easily allow them to better know and serve their customers.

Salesforce.com is a leader in the paradigm shift in software. The company's main product is a CRM (customer relationship management) software product, inexpensive and very easy to use. Plus, the company securely hosts the program, thus not tying up corporate database assets. Maintenance is minimal, the cost is a fraction of the older competitors' systems and the functionality is superb.

AQuantive is the leading company in the advertising/marketing space for the Internet. As companies move their advertising/marketing campaigns away from traditional media such as newspapers and television, aQuantive has both the technology and the expertise to set up, implement and monitor these campaigns.

Apple Computer, the iPod king, has revolutionized the MP3 player market, has dominant share and is supplying the content as well with their iTunes software. Apple's forward vision incorporates many applications including cell phone, video and general entertainment on the iPods. Apple has also branded the "Mac" computer. They're very strong in the consumer and educational space.

For a more detailed report on great growth ideas for 2006 and beyond, please refer to my website, www.stoplosingmoneytoday.com, where I discuss 20 to 25 ideas at any one time, with supporting documentation and what professional portfolio managers are doing and saying.

Find some great companies to invest in…and stop losing money!

## CHAPTER 9

## INVESTOR OR SPECULATOR?

THERE IS PROBABLY NOTHING MORE ANNOYING to me than hearing someone say, "Investing in the stock market is like Las Vegas—just roll the dice or pull the slot machine handle."

That statement just makes me quiver! Typically I hear it from someone who has been burned in the market and has a bad taste in their mouth. Unfortunately, some people do get burned, and the most overwhelming reason is that they have no plan or strategy and they don't do their homework.

We all have a cousin Bob or a buddy at work who hears that "XYZ is ready to go up big." My advice to you is, either walk away from cousin Bob or the work buddy, or do the homework!

### *A Hard Lesson Learned*

I once got burned on a "crapshoot" myself. Stupidly, I did no homework, no investigating, no checking out the research (which by the way, on this one, didn't exist!). I just bought it blindly. I found out about PowerHouse Technologies (PWHT.BB [or OB]—which means it is not NASDAQ listed, but on the NASDAQ bulletin board) from a co-worker who said that "smart" money was pouring into it, and it was the next big thing.

Wow! Gotta own the next big thing, right? And it was only a $1.50 per share! Man, this thing was ready to rumble. I bought 5,000 shares on the spot and thought, I'll check out the details later.

Well, later never came. I got busy, distracted—the usual. A month later I remembered this piece of %^$#@ and did check it out. The stock was at $0.40, as the "smart" money was getting out or had already gotten out.

What in the heck did I do and why? My co-worker of course was long gone, and I was sitting there holding the bag.

I still don't know what the heck this company even did! There is no point in even discussing that. The real point was I was speculating, not investing. I was hooked by the idea of "Wow, smart money is buying this one." I have yet to meet "smart money." I wonder what it looks like!

Speculating is exactly that: speculating. Typically it's a stock that no one's ever heard of, no real brokerage firm follows it or intends to and it's trading for pennies or a dollar or two. These speculative names tend to be one-trick ponies or hope to have one event that can carry the day. Or, they tend to have one product they're hoping works out well.

If this were a real company, many brokerage or investment banking firms would be bird-dogging it and providing it with sponsorship, which means a proper research report or a proper investment banker to advise them. I have seen companies that were quoted at pennies per share emerge, get real research and sponsorship, list accordingly on the NASDAQ and succeed.

However, the serious investors missed the move from $0.30 to $1—but so what? If the story has wheels to it, the real money will be made from $1 to $10.

An example is the company 24/7 Real Media (TFSM), which is in the Internet advertising/marketing sector. This company was pennies in 2004, but was really onto something, had decent technology and management, and wanted to be successful.

My firm did its homework and due diligence and agreed that TFSM had a future. We immediately recommended a reverse split of 1 for 10, meaning if you had 100 shares at $0.50, you then had 10 shares at $5 and a proper NASDAQ listing.

Many mutual funds cannot buy a stock unless it is listed on the New York Stock Exchange, The American Stock Exchange or the NASDAQ. TFSM has actually performed well and is trading at around $10.

The TFSMs do happen, but they are rare. Typically, speculative names remain as such and eventually go away. There is no fundamental basis to owning them. Speculative stocks trade at pennies for a reason: little or no revenues, no earnings and very few prospects. They tend to have minimal if any research and development efforts, and sales and marketing are probably nonexistent.

These companies are ignored by Wall Street because they have no prospect of emerging into the mainstream. So the next time cousin Bob or your work buddy come around with an idea, be wary.

## *Rolling the Dice*

Speculating can take on other forms that are also not so pretty, including the options market. Options have their place in properly hedging a portfolio, enhancing the yield of a stock or portfolio and balancing complex long/short strategies. Great, we got all that?

(These strategies are complex and typically, individual investors don't do them. Hedge funds and pension funds will implement these strategies, especially to protect on the downside.)

The straight-out buying of call options is speculative and can be dangerous, not to mention nerve-racking. A call option is the right to buy a stock at a specified price for a specified period of time—a privilege for which the customer pays a premium!

Example: XYZ is at $23 on May 6, and you feel it's going to run up nicely. Rather than buy 100 shares for $2,300, you buy one XYZ June 25 call option (one call option is worth 100 shares) and you pay a premium of $100.

Now, if XYZ trades up to $29 before the third Friday of June (expiration dates are always the third Friday of the month), great. Your option is now worth between $400 and $600. The reason for the range is the "time value." How much time is there before expiration?

At expiration, in this example, the option would be worth exactly $400, as the stock is at $29 and the "strike price" is at $25 and time has run out.

Where is the speculation here? If XYZ sits around $23 or goes down, or sits just under the $25 strike price, the option expires worthless. Zero! Now XYZ can jump to $27 after the third Friday of June, but the option has expired and is worthless. The person who owned the June 25 call was left holding the bag.

Option trading is truly speculative in nature. You own nothing but the "right" to buy that underlying stock, and time is against you. Again, I have some real-world experience here to show you what I mean.

In 1982, I was a third-year broker at Dean Witter Reynolds and life was good. I was making a good living and really enjoying my clients. Why would I screw that up?

I was a bit impatient and decided that I wanted to make some money quickly, so I speculated with options. There was an old company, Heublein, makers of A.1. Steak Sauce and other food products, that was rumored to be on the buy-out path (they were eventually bought out by Kraft

Foods). So, I bought some options and bingo, in two weeks I made $16,000.

Amazing and so easy…let's do it again! I bought some options in Clorox that didn't quite work out, but I lost only $500—no big deal. I bought some more, though for the life of me I cannot remember the company's name, and I was up $26,000 in total. I was a genius!

So, what do geniuses do? They go to Hawaii on vacation. I went with some friends, stayed at a fancy place, had some great food and drink—nothing but the best, right? Why not, I was a genius.

Yeah, well, I then proceeded to lose the entire $26,000 and then another $14,000. What a moron. Stop this train! I thought. I probably could have formed a club called Call Options Anonymous! I decided right then and there that I would never do it again—and I've stuck to it. I will never buy another call option.

What's the lesson? I was speculating in stocks without owning them and the clock was ticking. At the end of the day, I owned nothing. I was betting on an event to take place, or a piece of news to be announced. There was no ownership of the company and no fundamental work being done. Just events and news. Pure and simple speculating.

The worst thing that happened to me, and I have seen happen to others, is that I won the first time, and the second time, but it caught up with me because the odds were against me. It was not investing. I might as well have rolled the Vegas dice and had some fun doing it.

## Trading on Margin

This practice can either enhance your portfolio or devastate it. Margin, or borrowing money to own stocks, works this way:

you deposit, for example, $10,000 into your stock account, and the brokerage firm will allow you to buy up to $20,000 worth of stock—your $10,000 plus their $10,000.

The firm will then charge you interest on the borrowed funds, usually prime rate plus anywhere from 1.5 to 3.75 percent, depending on the loan size. The loan is collateralized by the stocks in the account. So far it's pretty simple, right?

So you own $20,000 worth of stocks; in six months they're worth $30,000. Nice job, great return. You sell your stock, pay back the brokerage firm the $10,000 plus some interest and walk away with nearly $20,000. On your $10,000 initial investment, you've just about doubled your funds. In rising bull markets, owning stocks on margin can enhance your returns.

But the opposite market action can really hurt. Back to our example: you own $20,000 worth of stock. You've put up $10,000 and borrowed ("margined") the other $10,000. The market takes a hard hit downward and your $20,000 is now worth $14,000. You decide to sell the stocks and pay off the margin debit.

You pay the firm its $10,000 and walk away with only $4,000. Ouch! Double whammy!

The bank, or in this case the brokerage firm, always gets paid first. There are federal rules that dictate margin requirements. All accounts on margin must maintain at least 25 percent equity or the firm must issue a federal maintenance call, which must be met within two business days with either cash or securities, or the brokerage firm is obligated by law to sell the appropriate value of stock to cover the "call."

The speculative use of margin is never wise. Federal calls are issued when invariably the market and/or the portfolio are at the worst point. I have seen accounts devastated during tough times because the "staying power" is not there to ride out the rough patches.

Accounts always get sold out right at the bottom. If the markets are strong and your stocks are participating, then margining your account can truly enhance your returns. But the moment you feel that the markets are turning south, either deposit cash or sell enough stock to eliminate the margin balance.

Remember this: in tough markets, the interest keeps adding up, the margin debit balance is always there and the supporting stock to carry the balance is declining in value. Not good. Get off margin as soon as possible.

In rising markets, returns can be accelerated, but watch the balance carefully and at the right moment, sell some stock and eliminate the margin debit. As an aside, you should know that brokerage firms love margin accounts because they are a very profitable business for them. The firms act just like banks, earning interest profits and controlling the collateral!

## What to Do With Charts

The other area of speculating that can drive you to drink is trading "on the charts." Every stock quoted has a chart that tracks the price and volume history for five minutes, for one day or all the way back, up to 10 years. Some charting services will track money flows, fancy trading bands, buy and sell signals (allegedly) and much more technical data.

I love charts. I look at them frequently. As they say, charts don't lie. Technical charts can demonstrate patterns and directions for stocks, show volume building to a breakout or breaking down, and often show where the near-term trading action is going.

Again, charts should be used as a tool, a source of information. I admit I look at the chart of a company immediately after I learn the ticker symbol. But I draw the line before buying or trading based solely on the chart action.

But some speculators do trade only off the patterns of the charts, fundamentals be damned. This is dangerous and they will eventually get burned beyond recognition. Why? Because when a company pre-announces a shortfall of revenues and/or earnings for a quarter or a year, the chart that may have been "pretty" all of a sudden becomes quite "ugly" and the profits are eviscerated. No fundamental work has been done or understood.

I have avoided pretty chart stocks because I understand that the fundamentals are in question, though they hadn't been announced or materialized yet.

The reverse is true as well. Great research can recommend a stock because the fundamentals have shifted positively, but the chart has not yet "confirmed" it. When the chart does confirm it, the first 30 percent gain may have been missed.

The pure chartist will say, "I thought maybe I was getting a head fake!"—an expression I've heard more than I care to remember. It's not a method to make good long returns on your capital. I'll emphasize it again: technical charts are important as a tool, but they do not take the place of solid research.

## Don't Take the Day Trading Bait!

"Day trading is the way to fast riches!" How many times did we all hear this in the late 90s and early 2000s? How many infomercials did we suffer through showing how "easy" day trading was? It was a joke.

My plumber, Ralph, told me in 2000 that he made $37,000 plumbing but made $61,000 day trading—and still he couldn't get my faucet to work right! Today, though, Ralph doesn't want to hear the words "day trading." He nearly goes into convulsions at the mere mention.

So I asked him, "What happened to your 'failproof' method and the guy you paid $995 to teach it to you?" Well, turns out the guy who taught Ralph is hiding—I mean living in Alaska somewhere.

Day trading was probably the most dangerous thing to happen to individual investors in the last 10 years. The technology was easy and affordable, and there were millions of Ralphs out there waiting to take the bait. Plus there were many "gurus" willing to share their methods for $995.

Day trading was based purely on price and volume movement. If a stock was up in the first hour of trading on heavier-than-normal volume, you bought it fast, looking to make 50 cents and then get out. If a stock was down in the first hour, same logic. It was all speculation and guessing.

It got to the point where professional market makers would "bid up" a stock at the open, knowing day traders would jump at it, and then the professional trader would purposely "drill it" back down. All this was accomplished within a range of 50 cents to 75 cents. It got to be a joke.

Compliance departments of the major brokerage firms gently asked the trading desks to cease and desist. Day trading seems to be a thing of the past, and let's keep it that way. Many people were hurt with this so-called strategy, but it was an almost sure way of losing money!

Investors with a strategy can sleep comfortably at night. Even if markets are going through a challenging time, if your strategy is well thought out and your broker or adviser is communicating and monitoring the investments with you, riding out the storm is fairly easy. If you are involved with a purely speculative investment, rough times will only get rougher. Investors invest; speculators play roulette.

And remember, the concept is to stop losing money today!

## CHAPTER 10

# THE MAGIC OF GROWTH INVESTING—
# FINDING YOUR APPROACH

LET'S BEGIN WITH THE PREMISE that businesses are built to grow. How many times have you heard a CEO say, "We would like to stay flat this year in both our revenues and profits?" Never! Any CEO with ideas like that would be looking for a new job!

Sometimes that happens as cycles dictate, but it is never planned for. The beauty of growth is that it is not constrained to our borders. Without going into a massive economics class or lesson, the fact is that our borders are becoming blurry. Our products and services play in the world markets, just as many other nations' products and services play in our nation. We almost forget that Heineken is a Dutch beer and that Toyota is a Japanese auto manufacturer.

It is certainly troubling to hear about General Motors laying off thousands of workers, or Ford Motors closing many US plants and people losing their jobs. But job growth in our nation continues upward. Yes, we have become a more services-oriented nation versus the old manufacturing base the United States enjoyed in years gone by.

So where do we look for growth and make our investments,

and when does growth investing become "value" investing, and when does "value" investing become growth?

## *Looking for Growth*

Each investor must define his or her definition of "growth." I look at what the return is on passive money, which is in a money market fund or US government 10-year bond, currently around 5 percent.

To me, growth is three to four times that rate, or 15 to 20 percent per year. Simple and clean, no confusion. If I can generate a consistent 15 to 20 percent return on my invested cash, I'm a happy investor. If I can generate more, I'm really happy!

More importantly, however, is generating that type of return over a five-year period. At 20 percent per year for five years, your funds will more than double. The trick is to do it, and do it consistently.

Historically, the markets will be very generous one year then very stingy the next. Remember the discussion about patience? 2003 was an excellent year, with growth funds and stocks returning nearly 30 to 40 percent, but 2004 was high single digits, as was 2005. But taking the average of the three years, returns hovered around 16 percent or so.

The industry where the US economy will continue to be strong, dominant and the world's leader is technology, both software and hardware. The software industry, taken as a whole—developers, implementers, retailers, code writers, the Internet—is the second largest industry in the United States. The automotive industry is still first, with all its attendant services and parts manufacturers, including tires.

I believe the source for this information was a crazy professor (beard, pipe and all) at the Wharton School of Business, where I attended an executive workshop for 3 weeks about 12 years ago. As that information is a bit old, I will assume that software has only gotten bigger and more widespread.

Other areas of definite growth in the United States are online educational services, business process services, wireless services, Internet media (including advertising and communications), medical devices, biotechnology and retailer/restaurant concepts.

The energy sector has acted well in the last two years, but this group will go in concert with the price of oil. If the price of oil holds in the $55 to $60 per barrel range, both current profits and exploration budgets will remain strong.

Notice I didn't say planes, trains and automobiles.

The stock market rewards companies that are simply growing their top line (revenue) and their bottom line (profits). Ultimately, this is the most important barometer for stocks going up in value.

The expectation of profits is also rewarded. This happens in emerging growth companies such as biotechnology and young software firms, but the actual profitability must materialize to justify any kind of actual premium in the shares.

Opsware (OPSW), remember, has a huge addressable marketplace, big-time loyal customers, a reduced selling cycle, mid-market and up-market product and dominance in the space, but eventually the profits must be present and growing. The current valuation of OPSW ($850 million market cap, and shares have doubled the past two years) is telling us that the market believes in all of the above and is giving the company a hefty valuation to prove it. Opsware now has to deliver, and then some.

## Investing in History

Let's talk about value investing and when value becomes growth. Typically a "value" company is one with a long history of delivering decent earnings and revenues, but for whatever reason seems to have hit a plateau where growth is stagnant.

Growth can be stagnant because of economic cycles or because the industry is out of favor. For example, look at Caterpillar Corp. (CAT)—a great American name, an illustrious history, maker of huge earth moving and construction equipment. One would argue that it's an old-world name, boring and lacking the sexiness we want in growth stocks.

Well, since late 2001, Caterpillar stock has four-folded, gone from about $20 to $80. Real boring, huh?

What happened? CAT struggled from 1996 to 2001; it didn't grow its top line and of course, the bottom line was stagnant as well. The stock was stuck in a trading range of $16 to $25 for those five years.

In 1999, CAT did $19.7 billion of revenues, 2000 revenues were $20.9 billion and 2001 revenues were $18.9 billion. During these three years, CAT was profitable and paid a decent dividend. Clearly this was a value stock. PE ratio was hovering around 8 to 13 times, and this great American company was certainly going to be around.

But would it emerge as a growth story? The value was clearly there. Beginning in 2002, CAT began to grow the top line, $20.1 billion; 2003, $22.7 billion; 2004, $30 billion; and 2005, $36.3 billion. The earnings went up commensurately, and the stock four-folded.

What were the catalysts to this value company's growth pattern? US and worldwide construction took off in 2001 and beyond, and CAT had positioned itself with a stronger dealer network, both in the United States and in Europe and Asia. The pieces were in place.

This information was available to all investors in 2001 but remember, at the time, it was boring and a "value play." It began to grow both top and bottom line and the stock acted like, smelled like, looked like and sure enough became a growth stock.

Now CAT will not perform as it has the past four years in the next four to six years (at least I don't think so!). Is construction (both US and world) slowing down? Has CAT taken its market share to the point where it's tough to grow?

If CAT encounters some of these issues, the stock will settle back and trade within a price range again for two to three years, and appear to be a value stock again. The company will continue to pay its dividend, earnings will continue to be solid, but will CAT continue to grow? The market doesn't reward stagnation with higher PE multiples.

The same analysis can be done for chemicals, utilities, automotive parts, financials and other industrial sectors. Growth will be cyclical in nature, but sustainability is another thing.

The other principle here is the law of large numbers. CAT is a good example of this. If they achieve their forecasted $38 billion of revenues for 2006 and grow just 10 percent ($3.8 billion ) for 2007, to a total of $41.8 billion—well, those are some large numbers indeed. This is possible but may be difficult; $3.8 billion is a lot of earth-moving equipment!

Many large companies get to the "plateau" where it becomes a huge challenge to keep top-line growth at double digits. They are solid, profitable companies that have stood the test of time. But they have already been rewarded in the market by their current market capitalization and, in many cases, their dividend yields. If you own companies like this, great, but where do you go from there?

## Finding Your Approach

I often hear the expression, "It's a great company" as a rationale to own the stock.

Stop right there! Let's accept the fact that CAT, GE and Microsoft are great companies and will withstand just about any economic cycle thrown at them, but as an investor, the more relevant question is: where do we go from here?

Judge these companies and begin the research process from ground zero. Ask what the growth rate is for the next three years. Can the company take additional market share in its space, or is its mission now to protect its own market share?

Yes, these old fogies are great companies, but where are they in their cycles? Microsoft has been stagnant for the last three years; stock performance has been mediocre. Oracle is desperately trying to acquire complementary software companies, as their own growth is stuck. The cycle they are stuck in is the law of large numbers, protecting their own market share and hopefully finding new growth initiatives.

In finding your approach, you may be comfortable holding on to some of the larger, more established companies. But to generate high growth returns to your portfolio, smaller to mid-cap names will be critical.

Currently, the two most valuable companies in the US stock market are ExxonMobile (XOM) at $395 billion market cap and General Electric (GE) at $355 billion. Wal-Mart (WMT) is at $194 billion, while Costco (COST) is at $25 billion.

I would rather own Costco, as it has a far better chance of growing to a $100 billion cap—a four-fold—than Wal-Mart has of going up to $800 billion. Costco is taking market share and expanding its club memberships, while Wal-Mart is trying to hold on to market share and show a little bit of growth.

Microsoft (MSFT) currently has a market cap of $282 billion, while Intuit (INTU) has a $9.6 billion cap and is growing like a weed. INTU has the chance to become a $25 billion to $30 billion cap name, while it will be challenging for MSFT to become $600 billion to $800 billion market cap.

Sure, Microsoft will right its course and probably grow again, but my personal portfolio growth would be better served with an INTU, an aQuantive or a Progressive Gaming

Corp. In finding your approach, remember to review the critical question of "where do we go from here?"

The GEs, MSFTs, XOMs and CATs are great companies, proven companies, but where do they go from here? You don't have to hit grand slams to win the game, but a couple of home runs will do just fine!

Finding your individual approach may be the mutual fund route. I would advise you to be as diligent in this area as you are in selecting a stock. I think there are now as many mutual funds available as there are individual company stocks.

## *Go for Experience, Not for a Name*

As we discussed earlier, the senior management of a company is the most important factor in making the buy or sell decision about a stock; the same is true for stock mutual funds. The senior portfolio manager is the most important factor. Period.

A stock mutual fund carrying a prestigious parent behind it, like Merrill Lynch, Citigroup or Fidelity, is unimportant. Who is running the money is far more important than who is marketing and administrating the mutual fund.

In looking at growth funds, I want a portfolio manager with at least five years' experience—preferably longer—with that fund or a similar one. Why? Because 2000 to 2006 have been tumultuous years—real wild rides. Did the portfolio manager run the funds in the late 90s go-go period and perform exceptionally well? Did she realize the bubble was going to burst and lighten up before it happened in late 2000 and early 2001?

Before buying into a fund, ask for the biography of the senior fund manager. How long has the portfolio manager worked this fund or similar funds? How did he fare during both good and bad times?

Example: I will not use his name as he is still running funds (which scares me), but I know a gentleman who rode the entire bubble down, refused to believe that valuations were being reset and finally sold many high-flying names at the bottom. Ouch!

Yet, he is still running money. I have nicknamed him Wrong-Way. He didn't think the energy group was sustainable and missed the entire move in 2005. I watch Wrong-Way carefully, as he is the polar opposite of which sectors are moving!

Wrong-Way is not currently involved in technology; he is "underweighted" in the sector, which by the way has done very well in fourth quarter 2005 and first quarter 2006. Wrong-Way still thinks WorldCom is coming back!

## *Look Back to Look Forward*

The returns on a stock mutual fund should be examined on a three-year basis. Why? Anyone can have a great, lucky year and conversely, anyone can hit a slump. Three years presents a balanced review of the stock funds' performance and, hopefully, direction.

Example: one fund I'm particularly fond of (full disclosure, I do own it myself) is the Calamos Growth Fund. Standard and Poor's ranking system currently has it at three stars out of five. So why get excited about a three-star ranking?

Peel back the onion a bit more and you'll see that Calamos has had a five-star ranking for the last 10 years, and a five-star ranking over the last five years. That is spectacular and consistent! Anyone can have a down year.

From 1995 to 2000, Calamos Growth Fund had returns from a high of 77 percent in 1999 to a low of 24 percent in 1997. But where the rubber meets the road is in the terrible years of 2001 and 2002. Calamos was down "only" 7.68 percent and 15.88 percent, respectively—in a period where some funds were dropping 40 to 50 percent.

In 2003, Calamos came back with a plus 42.4 percent return, again outperforming the market. For the 10-year period ending March 31, 2006, Calamos had an average annual return of 21.1 percent, versus a 9.2 percent average for all equity funds. That is stunning performance, but where do we go from here? Probably more of the same.

There is no reason for Calamos to underperform the next 3, 5 or even 10 years. Could it underperform this year or next? Sure, anyone can have an off year if their stocks just aren't playing as well or if they're underweighted in the sectors that are really moving and performing.

But with this particular fund, I know that the same portfolio manager and philosophy will prevail; the same mix of small, mid and large-cap names in the portfolio will also prevail.

There are many fine stock mutual funds, and a great source of information is Standard and Poor's mutual fund reports. The website is www.standardandpoors.com. Their research is thorough and independent. They are beholden to no one!

## *Sector Funds*

In finding your individual approach, I want to warn you about owning pure sector funds such as energy funds, medical and biotech funds and technology funds. Each sector has its days in the sun and conversely, each has its days in the doghouse.

I cannot tell you how many times I've heard an individual investor tell me, "I want to buy XYZ sector fund 'cause it had a great year last year." Remember, it's not what you don't own that's important, but what you do own or are going to own that's important. (Say that fast three times!)

Yes, XYZ sector fund had a great year last year, but where do we go from here? Energy had a terrific 2005 and early 2006, but it may be getting "rotated out" here in mid-2006. The overall performance may be just okay this year and possibly flat next year.

Sector funds limit the possibilities of being nimble and creative. Gold and precious resource funds will have a hot year or two, but then what? The key is to catch those funds when nobody else wants them.

Currently, if you want to own a sector fund, you may want to look at an alternative energy fund. This group is getting a lot of venture money behind it and portfolio managers are getting educated in this sector.

Another area that still has legs is the general technology sector. Corporate spending in technology hit the bottom in 2001 through 2004, thus stocks in technology performed horribly, but we are seeing corporate and government capital budgets moving back up to spend on technology. Biotechnology sector funds have done well; it may be time to look at them again in 2007.

All in all, sector funds are not like the Calamos Growth Fund, where the nimbleness of the portfolio team is in place and is allowed. Sector funds are exactly that: sectors. They do not allow for nimbleness to get out of or underweight any one group. They are the group!

## *The Big Picture*

Your approach to investing should be fun and challenging. The information that's available today to you, the individual investor, did not exist 10 to 15 years ago. Between company Websites, podcasts, Webcasts and good research available in many different venues like www.yahoo.com/finance, www.standardandpoors.com and www.cnnfn.com, your access to quality information is vast.

Still, the human touch is very necessary, so don't discount your broker or adviser. With the lessons taught back in Chapter 2: Trust…But Verify, you should be able to have a productive and profitable relationship with your broker(s).

I'm often asked, "What's your individual approach?" or "How do you manage your own money?" What I have written about in this book, I practice as well. I have three brokers, including myself. I do not have the market cornered on great ideas and perspective.

I have 65 percent of my liquid (non-real estate) assets in individual stocks, and 35 percent are in mutual stock funds. At age 51, I'm 14 to 17 years away from retirement, so all of my investments are in growth.

I will not be involved with bonds or fixed-income type investments. Why not? Simply, they do not grow. Sure, underlying bond prices will fluctuate with interest rate movements, but all in all, $1,000 in a bond will return $1,000. The fluctuations can vary as much as 10 to 20 percent up or down, but they do mature at $1,000. They do pay current income, normally twice a year, but I want to grow my capital.

Some will argue that I have all my eggs in one basket and am not diversified enough, but I think that's wrong. Aside from real estate, which in itself has grown incredibly in the last 10 years, the stocks or funds I own are diversified and in different industries. And no one stock makes up more than 7 percent of my portfolio, so if one were to become disastrous, it wouldn't affect the total portfolio that badly.

Plus, I'm a patient investor. As long as the fundamentals of a story are intact and the management team is executing to the stated public plan, I will wait it out.

I have owned Costco for seven years now. I have trimmed

it a bit, traded around a bit, but my core holding is still in the portfolio. There is no reason to sell this company. I bought aQuantive last year, in early 2005, and will probably hold it for the foreseeable future. If the story changes or a better mousetrap comes along, I'll sell it…because I don't love aQuantive, nor am I emotionally attached!

What about retirement? How should you adjust or move your holdings around?

Basically, I will move a bit more to dividend-paying stocks for some current income, but I will not ignore growth. I can envision a portfolio then of 50 percent growth, 35 percent growth with income, and 15 percent in cash or cash equivalents.

In finding your approach, it is important to understand what are you comfortable with. What do you want to achieve in your portfolio or net worth? You may be more comfortable with individual stocks making up 80 percent of your portfolio and mutual funds being the other 20 percent, or vice versa.

But have your strategy in place, have it understood by your advisers or brokers and implement it. Be nimble as well. If the story changes, go back and ask all the fundamental questions we discussed earlier in the book. After all, the idea is to stop losing money!

Investing should be fun and challenging. Keep in mind all the ideas and concepts discussed in this book. Keep your emotions to a minimum—but watch keenly for others' emotions. Trust…but verify. Be patient; think independently.

But, investigate and know when to buy, sell and buy more! Look around you; ask questions of people in different industries about what's new in their worlds. Check out company Websites, as they hold a lot of valuable information. These are a few ways to find great growth companies.

Identify your approach and your comfort level. Is it individual stocks or growth stock funds, or a combination of both?

Invest in companies or funds that you have good, quality information about; you want to leave your speculating to the tables in Las Vegas!

Above all else, have fun with this journey. As I mentioned earlier, I don't know where the markets will trade to in 2006 or 2007, and I don't believe anyone else knows either, but I do know and guarantee that the US equities markets will be more valuable 5, 10 and 15 years from now. Guaranteed!

So have fun…and stop losing money today!

# Epilogue

WRITING THIS BOOK and sharing the insights I have had the privilege of learning these past 27 years has been a pure joy.

I welcome you to come and visit my website at www.stoplosingmoneytoday.com and read my recommendations on the 20 to 25 stocks I currently like. The content will be a bit more detailed and informative about these companies. But I promise you the Website will be user- friendly!

I will outline these companies' market positions, addressable market sizes and growth rates; I'll discuss their managements' strengths and weaknesses; their competition; and of course, a price target.

The Website will also advise you when to buy, when to sell or when to buy more. I will conduct interviews with growth fund managers, what they see, what they like and what they don't like. I'm very fortunate, as I have access to some of the greatest research and smartest professional portfolio managers in the world.

Also, I will discuss the strengths of certain growth stock funds and growth and income funds.

Let's have some fun together and…stop losing money today!

# GLOSSARY OF TERMS

Analysts' ratings: A buy rating usually means that the analyst expects the stock to outperform the general market, so it is a good time to buy. A hold rating normally occurs after a company has missed a revenue and earnings expectation but the near-term prospects are still okay, so if you own the stock, you should hold it. A sell rating is exactly what it sounds like: sell it, as the near-term prospects look horrible and expectations for revenues and earnings will probably be lowered again and again.

**Back-end weighted:** Companies whose revenues typically come more in the back end of a quarter. For example, many software companies achieve up to 50 percent of their quarterly revenues during the last two weeks of the quarter.

**Basis point:** One basis point is equal to 1/100 of a percent. Example: 100 basis points equals 1 percent.

**Dead money:** Typically, when a company has badly missed revenue and earnings expectations and the stock has come way down in value and should stay down for 3 to 12 months, then the stock is called dead money.

**Initial price target:** The target price for a particular stock. Typically, the analyst, broker or individual investor should map out what the goal is of the investment by giving it a specific price target.

**Inside information:** Information about a company that is not available to the general public. It is not illegal to have inside information, but it is illegal if the information is acted upon.

**Insider insights:** Insights that are perfectly legal. They are general observations about a particular company or industry, such as identifying trends before they become mainstream, watching for pricing patterns in a product and if they are they rising or declining, and so on.

**IPO and IPO roadshow:** IPO means "initial public offering," which is when a private company will be offering its stock to the public for the first time. The roadshow is typically three to four-week, coast-to-coast meetings with professional portfolio managers.

**Market capitalization (market cap):** The total value of a publicly traded company. The formula is: all stock shares outstanding times the market price equals the market cap. Most professional portfolio managers describe micro-cap as a company with a market cap under $500 million, small-cap as under $2 billion, mid-cap as $2 billion to $10 billion and large-cap as above $10 billion.

**Net margin:** The after-tax profits of a company.

**Operating margin:** Probably the most important number that analysts and portfolio managers look for on a company's income statement. Operating margin is the money (profit) left over after ALL expenses, but before income taxes.

**PE:** Price-earnings ratio. The current stock price divided by the earnings per share. Example: stock is at $20 and earnings per share are $2, so $20 divided by $2 equals a PE of 10.

**PEG:** Price-earnings-to-growth ratio. In the above example the PE number is 10; divide that by the company's earnings growth rate, say 10 percent and you'll get a PEG of 1.

**Professional portfolio managers (also known as professional money managers, professional fund managers, or institutional money managers):** An individual or a small team of professionals whose sole job is to manage a portfolio. Typically, portfolios will have stated objectives, e.g., aggressive growth, general growth and growth with income.

**Ratable:** Companies whose revenues come in fairly evenly during the 12 weeks of a quarter. Example: restaurants, retailers and medical device companies.

**Retail broker:** A trained broker whose clientele is strictly individual investors and/or small businesses.

**SG&A:** Expenses associated in running a business in the selling, general and administrative areas.

**The Street:** The investment community normally made up of brokerage firms and investors, both individual and professional money managers.

**Technology tape:** Technology stocks generally trade up or down as a group, so it is referred to as the technology tape, or the tech tape.

**Ticker symbol:** Each publicly traded company is assigned a letter symbol to represent its name by either the New York Stock Exchange, The NASDAQ or the American Stock Exchange. Examples: Wal-Mart is WMT, General Electric is GE, Citigroup is C and Microsoft is MSFT.